The Official

Freebies

for

Families

Also available from Lowell House:
The Official Freebies® for Kids
The Official Freebies® for Teachers

The Official

Freebies

®

for
Families

Something for Next-to-Nothing for Everyone

By the Editors of *Freebies* Magazine
Illustrations by Will Suckow

Lowell House
Los Angeles

Contemporary Books
Chicago

Library of Congress Cataloging-in-Publication Data

Freebies for families / by the editors of Freebies magazine.
    p. cm.
    ISBN 1-56565-046-8
    1. Free material. I. Freebies (Santa Barbara, Calif.)
AG600.F75 1993
011'.03—dc20   92-34019
                                                      CIP

Requests for such permissions should be addressed to:
Lowell House
2029 Century Park East, Suite 3290
Los Angeles, CA 90067

Publisher: Jack Artenstein
Executive Vice-President: Nick Clemente
Vice-President/Editor-in-Chief: Janice Gallagher
Director of Publishing Services: Mary D. Aarons
Text Design: Brenda Leach

Manufactured in the United States of America

10 9 8 7 6 5 4 3 2 1

ABOUT THIS BOOK ....

Freebies For Families presents more than 250 *freebie* offers that you can get through the mail. The *Freebies* editors reviewed hundreds of offers before selecting the ones for this book. Each offer is written to describe the *freebie* as accurately as possible. Unlike other "get things free" books, ours includes only those suppliers who want to be listed and who have agreed to keep enough stock in inventory to honor all properly made requests.

HOW TO USE THIS BOOK ....

1. Follow the Directions: Each offer specifies how to order the *freebie*. Some offers specifically request a postcard (the Post Office will not process index cards in lieu of a postcard). Other offers may ask for an SASE (a long Self-Addressed Stamped Envelope with the requested postage). If a fee is requested, include the proper amount (a check or money order is usually preferred). Use a single piece of tape to affix coins. Some suppliers may wait for out-of-town checks to clear before honoring requests.

2. Print All Information: Not everyone's handwriting is easy to read. It is always safer to neatly print your name, address, and the complete spelling of your city on your request. Be sure to include your return address on your envelope or postcard. Use a ballpoint pen or a typewriter or computer to make your requests. Pencil often smears, and felt-tip pens easily smudge.

3. Allow Time for Your Request to Be Processed and Sent: Some suppliers send their offers via first-class mail. Others use bulk mail, which can take up to eight weeks. Our suppliers get thousands of requests each year, and processing time fluctuates depending on the time of the year.

4. What to Do if You Are Unhappy: If you are dissatisfied with an offer, let us know. If you have not received your offer within ten weeks of your request, let us know. Although we do not stock the items or offer refunds from our offices, we can follow up on your complaints with any supplier. Occasionally there are problems with a supplier or an offer. Your letters alert us to these problems. Suppliers who generate too many complaints will not be included in future editions. Send your complaints, comments, or suggestions to:

> Freebies Book Editors
> 1135 Eugenia Place
> Carpinteria, CA 93013

5. And There Is More: If you like the *freebie* offers you see in this book and want to see more great *freebies,* then you should subscribe to *Freebies* Magazine. Five times a year, *Freebies* sends you a great magazine with more than 100 *freebies* in each issue for only $8.95 a year. See the special offer on page 128.

ACKNOWLEDGMENTS ....

It is difficult to put together a book of this nature without the help of talented and dedicated people working together. The staff at Freebies has a special thanks for the commitment of RGA/Lowell House Publishing to this project. Their support made it happen.

Special thanks are reserved for Abigail Koehring, Margaret Koike, Don Weiner, and Linda Cook for the research, writing, and coordination of the material in this book.

Special mention must also be given to Bud Sperry, Janice Gallagher, Peter Hoffman, Mary Aarons, and the rest of the crew at RGA/Lowell House for the editing and design, and for the final push to complete the project.

Soitenly Stooges Memorabilia Catalog

MOE OFFERS FOR STOOGE FANS

The Three Stooges are as popular today as ever before. Larry, Moe, and Curly have become cultural icons for generations of fans who have followed the zany misadventures of this trio.

If you consider yourself an honorary stooge, you need to order this **catalog of memorabilia,** videos, books and other merchandise devoted to the Three Stooges.

Send: $2.00 postage & handling

Ask For: Soitenly Stooges catalog

Mail To: Soitenly Stooges, Inc.
P.O. Box 72
Skokie, IL 60076

Gem Consumer Kit

A REAL GEM

Selecting wedding rings is a serious proposal. Subtle differences in quality can greatly affect the value and price of a diamond. The American Gem Society has put together an informative **gem consumer kit** to educate customers on their jewelry selection.

It contains an 18-page, full-color booklet and a series of brochures that cover every facet of diamond shopping and provides a listing of North America's finest retail jewelers.

Send: Your name & address

Ask For: AGS Consumer Kit

Mail To: American Gem Society
Attention: Freebies
5901 West Third Street
Los Angeles, CA 90036-2898

● ● ● ● ● ● ● ● ● ● ● ● ● ● ● ● ●
Vitamin Booklet

DR. FOOD

Did you know that you'll feel warmer in winter if you have enough iron in your body? Or that B vitamins can prevent depression and anxiety? These are some of the facts you'll find in a fun booklet called *Test Yourself: How Many of These 100 Vitamin & Nutrition Tips Do You Know?*

This small, illustrated volume will surprise you with basic information on the role of nutrition in preventing and treating many health problems.

Send: Your name & address

Ask For: Booklet of 100 vitamin & nutrition tips

Mail To: Therapeutic Foods Nutrition Council
c/o H/K Communications
244 Madison Avenue
New York, NY 10016

● ● ● ● ● ● ● ● ● ● ● ● ● ● ● ● ●
Five Seed Packets

EDIBLE GARDEN

Grow a garden that will help your family fix fragrant, flavorful food; send for *five sample packets of herb seeds* plus planting instructions, recipes and a catalog that lists many more seeds that you can order. (The packets we received included basil, dill, chives, caraway and lemon balm.) What could be more satisfying than growing plants that will make memorable meals?

Send: $1.00 postage & handling

Ask For: Five sample packets of herb seeds

Mail To: Le Jardin du Gourmet
P.O. Box 75 D
St. Johnsbury Center, VT 05863

● ● ● ● ● ● ● ● ● ● ● ● ● ● ● ● ●

Microwave Tips
FAST FACTS

Everyone enjoys the speed and convenience of a microwave oven, but only a few people are adept at getting the most out of this popular kitchen appliance. There are many more uses for a microwave than popping corn or heating pizza. To learn how to get the most out of your microwave, send for this booklet containing **50 helpful hints.**

Send: $2.00 postage & handling

Ask For: Fifty microwave tips

Mail To: A.V. West
4627 Ashley Drive
Titusville, FL 32780

● ● ● ● ● ● ● ● ● ● ● ● ● ● ● ● ●

Air Freshener
WILDLY FRESH

Bring the outdoors indoors with an eye-catching, nose-pleasing **air freshener.**

Featuring a full-color reproduction of a wildlife painting by the famous artist Lee Cable, the double-sided cardboard air freshener measures 2-3/4" x 3-3/4".

Hanging from its elastic cord, the scented ornament will impart a clean, outdoorsy fragrance to your car, bathroom, den, or kitchen.

Send: $1.25 postage & handling

Ask For: Air freshener

Mail To: Sav-on
Dept. A
P.O. Box 1356
Gwinn, MI 49841

Alarm Stickers

QUITE A SCARE

Play it safe: request these **four alarm stickers** that help deter unwanted visitors from breaking into your home. Place the blue-and-white decals in strategic spots near doors and large windows. Then potential burglars can't help but notice the stickers, which announce, "Warning: Protected 24 Hours by Automatic Electronic Alarm System."

Send: $1.00 postage & handling

Ask For: Four house alarm stickers

Mail To: S. Brown
P.O. Box 568
Techny, IL 60082

Alaskan Photo Cards

WILD THINGS

If you've ever dreamed of visiting wild Alaska, then you'll want to send for these **four Alaskan photo cards** that depict life on our last American frontier. Captured by photographer Steve Fretwell, the subjects include a grizzly bear, a moose, Canadian geese, and a musher with his sled dogs. Accompanied by envelopes and attached to 4-1/2" x 6" note cards, the full-color photos will have you packing your bags immediately.

Send: $1.50 postage & handling

Ask For: Four Alaskan photo cards

Mail To: Alaska Craft
Dept. NP/S
Box 11-1102
Anchorage, AK 99511

• • • • • • • • • • • • • • • • •

Booklet

EVERYTHING'S COMING UP ROSES

No other group of plants has the loyal following enjoyed by the rose. It is the most readily recognized, widely grown and deeply loved of all flowers. This **16-page full-color booklet** on the care and selection of award-winning roses is a must for every rose enthusiast. It also includes landscape ideas and tips on how to shop for the plants.

Send: $1.00 plus a long SASE

Ask For: *All-America Rose Selections* booklet

Mail To: All-America Rose Selections
Dept. FB
221 North LaSalle Street, Suite 3900
Chicago, IL 60601

• • • • • • • • • • • • • • • • •

Bracelet Kits

STRING-A-LONG

Say it with feeling; say it with beads. String **your** thoughts or your favorite names on elastic and **wear** them for all to see. Send for **three alphabet bracelet kits** and express yourself clearly—and have fun doing so.

Each kit comes with 40 alphabet beads, 36 assorted colored beads, and elastic thread so that you can bead creative.

Send: $2.00 postage & handling for three kits

Ask For: Three alphabet bracelet kits

Mail To: Who's Who Baby
8858 El Capitan
Fountain Valley, CA 92708

Cat Care Pamphlet

FEEDING YOUR FELINE

Cats have a bad reputation as picky eaters, but they might not be so finicky if their owners realized that cats prefer their meals to be served at room temperature.

This pamphlet is a complete **owner's manual for cat lovers,** covering everything from housebreaking to health precautions. It's true that felines are among the most self-reliant house pets, but they still need your help from time to time.

Send: A long SASE

Ask For: *Cat Care and Feeding* pamphlet

Mail To: The American Feline Society, Inc.
204 West 20th Street
New York, NY 10011

Magazine

FOCUS ON CAGE-BIRDS

Few things are more colorful than the wide array of cage-birds available to pet owners. But this magazine devoted to bird owners comes in a close second.

Filled with articles, full-color photos, and illustrations, each edition of *American Cage-Bird* **magazine** will be a welcome treat for enthusiasts. Send in for a sample copy and enjoy articles on varying subjects from cockatoos to canaries.

Send: $2.00 postage & handling

Ask For: Sample copy of *American Cage-Bird* magazine

Mail To: *American Cage-Bird* Magazine
One Glamore Court
Dept. B-7
Smithtown, NY 11778

Cat Lovers' Catalog

GIFTS FOR CAT OWNERS

Cat lovers will be interested in this **catalog and sample card** of original greeting cards, limited edition prints and other top quality gifts all featuring their favorite felines. The card you will receive will be a special card to use for Thanksgiving.

This catalog is chockfull of gift ideas for every occasion from Christmas to birthdays. Better yet, you may just find something you want to keep for yourself.

Send: $2.00 postage & handling

Ask For: Cat Lovers' catalog and sample card

Mail To: Art Studio Workshops
518 Schilling
Dept. THS
Forest Lake, MN 55025-1038

Luggage Label

BAG TAG

Here's the perfect personalized gift to give a friend or relative: a laminated **luggage tag** made from two of his or her business cards. Measuring 2-1/2" x 4-1/2", the label has a 5" black vinyl strap that allows its owner to attach the tag to a briefcase, suitcase, or any kind of luggage.

Send: $1.75 postage & handling plus two identical business cards or printed name and address

Ask For: Luggage tag

Mail To: S. Brown
P.O. Box 568
Techny, IL 60082

• • • • • • • • • • • • • • • • • •

Bee Pollen Information & Sample

BEEHIVE MEDICAL MIRACLES

Ever since the time of ancient Egypt and Greece, mankind has known of the special nutrition and medicinal qualities of honeybee pollen. If you're unaware of the many benefits derived from pollen, then this **brochure and sample** will give you a thorough overview on the subject. It also includes a suggested pollen program to help you put a little buzz back in your life.

Send: $1.00 postage & handling

Ask For: Bee pollen information & sample

Mail To: Golden Pride/Rawleigh
3408 Heyward Street
Columbia, SC 29205

• • • • • • • • • • • • • • • • • •

Beekeeper Catalog

TAKE THE STING OUT OF BEEKEEPING

Beekeeping is not only an interesting hobby, but a profitable one as well. However, it does require proper equipment to produce high-quality beeswax and honey. The one place to find such items is this **full-color catalog**, which includes everything from hives to protective garments. It also lists a number of instructional books and videos to get you started.

Call: 1-800-637-7468

Ask For: Beekeeper catalog

• • • • • • • • • • • • • • • •

Buttermilk Sample

BETTER WITH BUTTERMILK

Inside a chocolate cake or atop buttered biscuits you might expect to find something fattening. Cultured Buttermilk Blend is a savory surprise that is low in calories and gives great taste with virtually no fat or cholesterol. It is also a rich source of calcium.

With this free offer, you'll receive a **1-oz. sample of SACO® real Cultured Buttermilk Blend,** a collection of fat-fighting recipes and helpful hints for a healthier diet, money-saving coupons.

Send: Your name & address

Ask For: Buttermilk Powder sample

Mail To: SACO Foods/Dept. F
P.O. Box 616   Or call toll-free:
Madison, WI 53562   1-800-373-SACO

• • • • • • • • • • • • • • • •

Newsletter

SWEEPSTAKES SECRETS

Envision yourself on a New York shopping spree or a Caribbean cruise. Imagine yourself winning big in a sweepstakes.

Now do something about that dream. Request a current **Big Money Sweepstakes Newsletter** and find out about upcoming sweepstakes that offer valuable prizes.

The eight-page newsletter provides information on how and when to enter these "big money" contests.

Send: $2.00 postage & handling

Ask For: Current issue of *Big Money Sweepstakes Newsletter*

Mail To: *Big Money Sweepstakes Newsletter*
P.O. Box 221033-FB
Chantilly, VA 22022

Home Security Booklet
PROPERTY PROTECTION

Defend your home and hearth from unlawful entry; lock doors and windows whenever you leave, and request a copy of the helpful 10-page **booklet called** *Bless This House: A Home Security Audit.* Then read and follow the booklet's advice on securing your home inside and out and organizing a neighborhood watch system.

Send: Your name & address

Ask For: *Bless This House: A Home Security Audit*

Mail To: Aetna Resources
151 Farmington Avenue, RWAC
Hartford, CT 06156

Blindness Catalogs, Newsletters & Information
SUPPLIES FOR THE SIGHTLESS

Living with blindness isn't easy. A wide range of reading and learning materials is available to the sightless, as well as similar items for their family and friends.

The American Printing House for the Blind has catalogs, newsletters, and **informational material** that it will send you upon request. You'll receive a catalog of Braille publications, a catalog of instructional aids and supplies, and a special braille edition of *My Weekly Reader* to show children how their sightless friends read.

Send: Your name & address

Ask For: Catalogs & newsletters and a braille edition of *My Weekly Reader*

Mail To: American Printing House for the Blind
P.O. Box 6085   Or call toll-free:
Louisville, KY 40206   1-800-223-1839

●●●●●●●●●●●●●●●●●

Booties Pattern

DO THE SOFT SHOE

Soften the pitter patter of little feet or warm the toes of your favorite infant. Follow this **infant booties pattern** and create soft fabric shoes in three different sizes.

The accompanying instructions make the booties a fast and easy project that results in an economical, thoughtful gift.

Send: $1.75 postage & handling

Ask For: Infant booties pattern

Mail To: Little People's Patterns
P.O. Box 713
Thornton, WA 99176

●●●●●●●●●●●●●●●●●

Candy Sample

IT BUTTER BE GOOD

"This is the best darn candy you ever slung a lip over," boasts Uncle Zeke of his confectionery. That crusty old Zeke has been making his own butterscotch candy up in Maine since most folks can remember. Now his niece has also taken to cooking up batches of the sweet treat at her kitchen high in the Sierra Nevadas to share with all of us candy lovers.

True to Zeke's 150-year-old recipe, only the finest natural ingredients are used. So try a **sample of Uncle Zeke's™ Old Fashioned Cracked Butterscotch.** You're sure to love it and want more once it's gone.

Send: A long SASE

Ask For: Butterscotch sample

Mail To: Uncle Zeke's
401 Village Boulevard
Incline Village, NV 89451

Wild Rice Recipes

A WILD SIDE DISH

California wild rice makes a great side dish for your next meal. Here's a variety of ways to prepare this healthy gourmet grain. You can stuff an artichoke with it or make wild rice clam chowder. These **recipes** include a listing of all nutritional values. Wild rice is low in calories but high in vitamins.

Send: A long SASE

Ask For: California wild rice recipes

Mail To: California Wild Rice Recipes
335 Teegarden
Yuba City, CA 95901

Recipe Booklet

STRAWBERRY DELIGHTS

Strawberry shortcake and fresh strawberry pie are just two ways to enjoy this tasty fruit. Did you ever think about making strawberry pizza or strawberry chicken salad? Recipes for these and other culinary creations abound in this **booklet** devoted to the California strawberry. There are also important tips on how to select the best strawberries at the fruit stand.

Send: $1.00 postage & handling

Ask For: Strawberry recipe booklet

Mail To: A Basket of Fresh Ideas
The California Strawberry Advisory Board
P.O. Box 269
Watsonville, CA 95077-0269

Cat Handbook

CARE FOR CATS

If felines are your friends, *The Cat Care Handbook* can provide authoritative tips on promoting the health and happiness of your own furry companion.

Packed with articles on moving cats to a new house, introducing baby to kitty, choosing pet sitters, and more, the 36-page, illustrated **booklet** entertains and informs.

Send: $1.00 postage & handling

Ask For: *The Cat Care Handbook*

Mail To: Dept. ILC
Grass Roots Publishing
950 Third Avenue, 16th Floor
New York, NY 10022

Pierced Earrings

COOL CATS

Cat lovers, jewelry collectors, and pewter enthusiasts, take note. This delightful pair of **cat-face earrings** makes a wonderful gift or stocking stuffer.

Made in the United States, the pierced earrings each sport a stylized, smiling cat face cut from pewterlike metal.

Send: $2.00 postage & handling

Ask For: Pewter-tone cat-face earrings

Mail To: Marsha Patterson
P.O. Box 2428
Melbourne, FL 32902

Cats Magazine Sample Copy

KEEPING UP ON KITTY

Cat lovers will rejoice when they order a sample copy of this colorful, high-quality monthly publication devoted to felines. They'll enjoy the many photos, the informative departments, and the variety of feature articles. **Cats Magazine** also comes chock-full of classified ads from breeders and listings of future cat shows around the country.

Send: $1.00 postage and handling
Ask For: Sample issue of *Cats Magazine*
Mail To: *Cats Magazine*
              P.O. Box 290037
              Port Orange, FL 32129

Child Care Information

ASK FIRST

Whether to provide their children with in-home care or group care is not an easy choice for working parents to make. Where you leave your child is a decision that should be made with care and thought. Many parents must pick a professional child-care provider, and this free **pamphlet, *Child Care: What's Best for Your Family,*** is an important aid in helping you make the right choice. Easy to read and easy to use—a checklist of items to look for and questions to ask is provided—this is an invaluable aid for all parents.

Send: A long SASE
Ask For: *Child Care: What's Best for Your Family* brochure
Mail To: American Academy of Pediatrics (AAP)
              Publications Dept.
              P.O. Box 927
              Elk Grove Village, IL 60009

• • • • • • • • • • • • • • • • • •
Safety Folder

FACTS ON FILE

In an emergency, would you be able to rattle off all pertinent facts about the health and appearance of your child?

This sturdy, six-panel **Child File** might make talk unnecessary. The 3-1/4" x 7" folder offers places to list and diagram your child's physical characteristics, a spot to attach a current photo, and even ink and a chart on which to fingerprint your child.

Send: $1.50 postage & handling

Ask For: Child File

Mail To: Special Products
Dept. FB
P.O. Box 6605
Delray Beach, FL 33484

• • • • • • • • • • • • • • • • • •
Auto Decals

SAFE ON BOARD

As a kid, when you wanted some attention you kicked up a fuss or started an argument, right? Well, here's a better way for your children to get noticed when you're on the road; it's a **set of two "Child on Board!" stickers** that will adhere to your car.

Most importantly, these four-inch square decals, which are printed on reflective plastic, will notify emergency workers that your children are in the car should you have problems on the road.

Send: $1.00 postage & handling for two

Ask For: Two "Child on Board!" stickers

Mail To: Neetstuf/Dept. F2-14
P.O. Box 459
Stone Harbor, NJ 08247

Bag Pattern

KID'S CARRY-ALL

Construct a kid-size, multipurpose fabric bag for carrying coloring books, crayons, toys, puzzles, and general treasures. Simply send for these **Child's Carry-All Bag instructions** and choose some sturdy fabric (like ticking) plus a few fabric paints.

The directions are easy, and you can enlarge the dimensions to create a diaper bag or a mom's tote.

Send: $1.50 postage & handling

Ask For: Child's Carry-All Bag instructions

Mail To: Little People's Patterns
P.O. Box 713
Thornton, WA 99176

Vision Pamphlets

KEEP AN EYE OUT

...for potential vision problems in young children. According to *Your School-Age Child's Eyes* and *Your Preschool Child's Eyes,* parents and teachers need to be alert for symptoms that may indicate a child can't see properly.

The two brochures advise parents not to rely on vision screenings and to seek good optometric care. The publications also offer tips on how best to protect a child's eyes during play and TV viewing.

Send: A long SASE

Ask For: *Your School-Age Child's Eyes* and
Your Preschool Child's Eyes

Mail To: Communications Center
American Optometric Association
243 North Lindbergh Boulevard
St. Louis, MO 63141

• • • • • • • • • • • • • • • • •

Sample Copy of Children's Publications

GREAT READING FOR KIDS

No question it's important to develop good reading habits in your children, and there's no better way to do that than with a **publication written especially for kids.**

You can receive a sample copy of any one of the following six titles: *Turtle Magazine* (preschoolers), *Humpty Dumpty* (kindergarten age), *Children's Playmate* (six to eight year olds), *Jack & Jill* (seven to ten year olds), *Child Life* (intermediate readers), and *Children's Digest* (preteens).

Send: $1.25 each for each title

Ask For: The magazine(s) by title

Mail To: Children's Better Health Institute
1100 Waterway Boulevard
Attn: Jeanne Aydt, Sample F
Indianapolis, IN 46206

• • • • • • • • • • • • • • • •

Camp Brochure

PICK A PERFECT PLACE

Kids develop their self-esteem, social skills, and knowledge of the great outdoors when they enroll in one of the 8,500 day and residents camps in the United States.

This **brochure, titled *How to Choose a Camp for Your Child,*** guides parents as they try to select just the right camp for their children—or for their entire family. The eight-panel publication also lists books and services.

Send: A long SASE

Ask For: *How to Choose a Camp for Your Child* brochure

Mail To: Free Brochure
American Camping Association
5000 State Road 67 North
Martinsville, IN 46151

Hanger Kit

WHAT A CIRCUS

We'll bet your kids will pick up their clothes more often if you make them special, kid-size wooden hangers from this **Circus Happy Hanger pattern,** which includes complete instructions and full-size blueprint patterns to produce clown, monkey, and cowboy hangers.

The pattern also comes with a catalog and a half-price coupon for other terrific wood project patterns.

Send: $1.00 postage & handling

Ask For: Circus Happy Hanger pattern plus catalog and coupon

Mail To: Design Group
Box 514-FB
Miller Place, NY 11764

Sample Issue

BIG-TOP NEWS

Get on the bandwagon and send for this entertaining, educational tabloid called **Circus Tails.** Published by Circus World Museum in Baraboo, Wisconsin, the town where Ringling Brothers Circus began in 1884, the eight-page publication presents fascinating articles about circuses and their history. The tabloid also includes puzzles, games, and coloring activities geared for children in elementary school.

Send: Your name & address

Ask For: Complimentary issue of *Circus Tails*

Mail To: *Circus Tails*
c/o Circus World Museum
426 Water Street
Baraboo, WI 53913-2597

Cloud Chart

SKY HIGH

Clouds, whether they're fluffy and puffy or streaky and thin, can help us forecast the weather. That's why this 11" x 17" **cloud chart** is so fascinating and useful.

With its full-color photo chart and detailed information, the chart (which comes in two different comprehension levels) will have children and adults checking the wind and watching the clouds for sky-high signs of the weather to come.

Send:	$2.00 postage & handling
Ask For:	Cloud Chart (specify chart C for grades three to five or chart B for grades six and up)
Mail To:	Cloud Chart P.O. Box 21298 Charleston, SC 29413

Cocoa Butter Soap

BAR NONE

Handmade using the time-consuming kettle method, this **full-size bar of Simmons cocoa butter soap** may be the finest soap you've ever tried, bar none.

Weighing about four ounces and enriched with vitamin E, this completely biodegradable soap soothes skin that has suffered from harsher soaps. Its superior ability to moisturize derives from extra doses of natural oils and pure tallow.

Send:	$2.00 postage & handling
Ask For:	One full-size bar of Simmons Cocoa Butter Soap
Mail To:	Simmons Pure Soaps 42295 Highway 36, Dept. F Bridgeville, CA 95526

● ● ● ● ● ● ● ● ● ● ● ● ● ● ● ● ●

Information Flyer

A Sporting Chance

Sports trading cards are no longer kids' stuff. They constitute a major industry that grosses millions every year and entices international investors.

Now you can turn your love of these collectibles into a part- or full-time business. Find out how by sending for a six-page **information flyer from The Collectors.**

Send: A long SASE

Ask For: Information flyer about Collectors II International Sports Series

Mail To: The Collectors
26 Broadway
Beverly, MA 01915-4437

● ● ● ● ● ● ● ● ● ● ● ● ● ● ● ● ●

Book & Magnet

Fire Fighters

Children accidentally set many of the burn-causing fires in our country because they see fire as a toy rather than a tool. Grownup Americans could avert at least half of all burn accidents if they made a few changes in their homes and habits.

This 42-page *Color Me Safe* **coloring book** and flexible, 4" x 7" **"Be Safe From Fire and Burns" magnet** will help you and your family fight fires by preventing them in the first place.

Send: $1.00 postage & handling for the coloring book; $1.00 postage & handling for the magnet

Ask For: *Color Me Safe* coloring book and/or "Be Safe" magnet

Mail To: National Institute for Burn Medicine
909 East Ann Street
Ann Arbor, MI 48104

• • • • • • • • • • • • • •

Materials Catalog

CONE CRAFTS

Pinecones provide the perfect inspiration for dozens of craft projects. This wholesale **handicraft materials catalog** includes a bonus four-page section with 37 craft projects using pinecones and seashells. Dozens of wholesale-priced handicraft materials fill the rest of the 80 pages.

Send: $1.00 postage & handling

Ask For: Handicraft materials catalog

Mail To: Creative Craft House
P.O. Box 2567
Dept. F
Bullhead City, AZ 86430

• • • • • • • • • • • • • •

Catalog of Free or Low-Cost Booklets

CONSUMER INFORMATION

The United States General Services Administration has a very active **Consumer Information Center.** It has prepared more than 200 booklets on money, children, and other consumer concerns. Now those booklets, which are either free or extremely low-cost, are listed in one catalog.

Whether you desire information on nutrition, education, or federal programs, you'll find the right booklet in this catalog.

Send: Your name & address

Ask For: Consumer information catalog

Mail To: Consumer Information Catalog
Pueblo, CO 81009

Canned Fruit Recipes

A PEACHY DEAL

Sweeten your menus and simplify your life with nutritious canned fruits. Send for **consumer recipes and nutrition information on canned fruits.**

Cook up a batch of pear chutney, toss a fruited spinach salad, or have your teenager whip up his own peachy California fruit cooler.

Send: A long SASE

Ask For: Consumer recipes and nutrition information on canned fruits

Mail To: Canned Fruit Promotion Service
Attn: FREE
P.O. Box 7111
San Francisco, CA 94120

Whale teaching kit

START A WHALE MIGRATION

When your child is bored, you could say you have a whale of a problem. Take care of it with this **Whales of the World Teaching Kit.** Your child's attention will immediately migrate toward this interesting subject as you engage him or her in fun activities.

The kit includes nine lessons with activity sheets, a glossary, and a guide. It is appropriate for children of all grade levels and ages. Also in the kit, you will find information on how you can adopt a whale through the nonprofit Whale Adoption Project.

Send: $1.00 postage & handling

Ask For: Whales of the World Teaching Kit

Mail To: Whale Adoption Project
P.O. Box 388
North Falmouth, MA 02556-0388

• • • • • • • • • • • • • • •

Crochet Instructions

CREATURE COMFORTS

Has your child outgrown her favorite comfy slippers? Then send for these **crochet instructions for country animal slippers in four sizes** and create a pair of bunny, lamb, kitty, or puppy slippers that will please her feet.

Because the instructions cover four sizes, from toddler to adult, the rest of the family can slip into some snuggly slippers, too.

Send: A long SASE

Ask For: Crochet instructions for country animal slippers

Mail To: Lorraine Vetter—CPF
7924 Soper Hill Road
Everett, WA 98205

• • • • • • • • • • • • • • •

Strawberry or Spruce Seeds & Growing Instructions

A GARDENER'S CHOICE

Before spring arrives and you finalize plans for planting a garden, you might want to send off for these **seeds and a growing guide.**

You can order seeds for two everbearing strawberry plants and/or a seedling for a blue spruce evergreen tree. Both come with complete growing instructions. And if you get started early, the blue spruce evergreen can be used as a Christmas tree next year.

Send: $1.50 for strawberry plants
$2.00 for blue spruce evergreen

Ask For: Two strawberry plants and/or
One blue spruce evergreen

Mail To: Country Heritage Nurseries, Inc.
P.O. Box 536
Hartford, MI 49057

Catalog

SUPPLIES CACHE

Collectors of stamps, coins, baseball cards, and post-cards will want to collect this comprehensive **Collectibles & Supplies catalog,** which lists all the fun paraphernalia that makes your hobby so rewarding.

The publication allows you to shop through the mail for items that will help you sort, display, and assess your collection.

Send: 75 cents in postage stamps

Ask For: Collectibles & Supplies catalog

Mail To: Crafts & Collections
P.O. Box 291
Portland, CT 06480

Catalog & Card

LEARN BY DOING

The unique **Creative Learning Products catalog** will immerse you in colorful photos of kids from 18 months to 12 years old enjoying hands-on experience with paper projects. The catalog offers child-oriented place mats, costumes, calendars, workbooks, stationery, and educational videos.

With the catalog you'll also receive a bookmark, a blank note card, and an application for the free "Kards for Kids" Fun Club.

Send: $1.00 postage & handling

Ask For: Note card, bookmark, Fun Club application and Creative Learning Products catalog

Mail To: Creative Learning Products, Inc.
3567 Kennedy Road
South Plainfield, NJ 07080

• • • • • • • • • • • • • • • • • •

Booklet

CREDIT TO YOU

When economic times are tough, many folks begin to rely on credit too heavily.

How to Be Credit Smart, a 12-page booklet published by the government, provides guidelines for responsible credit use and outlines steps to take if problems arise. It also includes important information about how to obtain, use, and benefit from credit.

Send: A long SASE

Ask For: *How to Be Credit Smart* booklet

Mail To: Consumer Credit Education Foundation
919 18th Street, NW, Third Floor
Dept. CS
Washington, DC 20006

• • • • • • • • • • • • • • • • • •

Safety Brochure

CRIB CAUTIONS

Each year more than 13,000 children are seriously injured in crib accidents, and about 65 children die. Parents could prevent many such injuries by making sure that their child's crib meets the guidelines listed in this detailed, six-page brochure titled ***Is Your Crib Safe?***

So before you acquire a new or used crib, be sure to read this important publication, which warns against dangerous corner posts, poor mattress fit, slat width greater than 2-3/8" and other hazards.

Send: A long SASE

Ask For: *Is Your Crib Safe?* brochure

Mail To: The Danny Foundation
P.O. Box 680
Alamo, CA 94507

Reproduction Print

FOR THE HORSEY SET

Fans of Currier & Ives, the renowned 19th-century print makers, or of harness racing, will want to trot out their pens and paper and request this 5" x 7" reproduction of the **Currier & Ives print** *Trotting for a Great Stake* from 1896.

Offered by the Trotting Horse Museum, this glossy print shows three sleek trotters pulling their drivers in the lightweight, two-wheeled sulkies that were popular at the turn of the century.

Send: $2.00 postage & handling

Ask For: 5" x 7" reproduction of the Currier & Ives print
Trotting for a Great Stake
(catalog of other prints and horse-related items also available upon request)

Mail To: Trotting Horse Museum
P.O. Box 590
Goshen, NY 10924

Enzyme Drops

SMELL OF SUCCESS

Dogs and cats often exhibit a condition not even their owners are willing to discuss: flatulence—gas—from undigested complex sugars in their intestines.

A new product offers a solution to this sometimes offensive problem. Pleasant-tasting **CurTail™ Drops,** when added to a pet's food, improve the digestibility of the complex sugars that many pet foods contain.

This will last for up to 12 feedings.

Call: 800-257-8650 between 8:30 A.M. & 9:30 P.M. EST

Ask For: CurTail Drops sample

• • • • • • • • • • • • • • • • • •

Nutrition Booklets

VERY DAIRY GOOD

Babies don't come with feeding instructions, so the National Dairy Council publishes booklets.

The council's **Airplane, Choo-Choo & Other Games Parents Play** is a "feeding guide for the first two years." **The All-American Guide to Calcium-Rich Foods** offers guidelines for choosing foods rich in calcium, necessary for strong bones and for the health of our muscles, heart, blood, and nervous system.

Send: $1.00 postage & handling plus a long SASE

Ask For: *Games Parents Play* &
The All-American Guide to Calcium-Rich Foods

Mail To: National Dairy Council   Dept. KD
O'Hare International Center
10255 West Higgins Road, Suite 900
Rosemont, IL 60018

• • • • • • • • • • • • • • • • •

Instruction
Booklet

CRAFTY IDEAS

Decorate your home economically and even ingeniously; send for a copy of **Crafts for the Home,** a 32-page collection of creative projects.

Published by *Decorating Digest,* the booklet offers clear, easy instructions for such techniques as wall stenciling; turning silk flowers into porcelain; and assembling pillow, table, and furniture covers without sewing a stitch.

Send: $1.00 postage & handling

Ask For: *Crafts for the Home*

Mail To: Crafts for the Home
Dept. DD/Grass Roots Publishing
950 Third Avenue, 16th Floor
New York, NY 10022

Sugar-Free Candy Catalog

SWEET LUXURIES

If you have an affection for confections but can't eat sugar, you'll hanker to order everything in **Delty's catalog of sugar-free chocolates and candy.** Filled with full-color photos of delectable treats, the 5-1/2" x 8-1/2" catalog features candy sweetened with such ingredients as fruit juices, fructose, cornstarch derivatives, and mannitol.

Now even diabetics can splurge on sweets.

Send: Your name & address, or call 1-800-962-3355

Ask For: Delty's catalog of sugar-free chocolate candy

Mail To: Delty Sugar-Free Chocolate
Dept. F
412 North Coast Highway, No.356
Laguna Beach, CA 92651

Cross-stitch Designs

TAILOR-MADE TOWELS

An easy way to add a decorative touch to your bathroom is to cross-stitch designs or your initials on hand towels. That job is made easier with the help of the 12 designs and complete alphabet sampler available in this helpful **booklet.**

You'll find colorful designs that can be used on all types of linens, along with complete instructions. There is also a color conversion chart to help you pick out the correct thread.

Send: $1.00 postage and handling

Ask For: Towels to Treasure

Mail To: Designs by Harry D.
227 North Stonehedge Drive
Columbia, SC 29210

• • • • • • • • • • • • • • • • • •

Newsletter

JET-SET DIABETICS

Travel is an opportunity for personal growth, but it can disrupt the regimens of some diabetics.

The quarterly **Diabetic Traveler** is a six-page, well-researched newsletter that helps such folks plan safe, secure travel.

Request a sample issue and also receive a wallet-size **insulin adjustment guide for jet travelers.**

Send: $1.00 postage & handling plus a long SASE

Ask For: Sample issue of *The Diabetic Traveler* plus Insulin Adjustment Guide

Mail To: *The Diabetic Traveler*
P.O. Box 8223-RW
Stamford, CT 06905

• • • • • • • • • • • • • • • • •

Discover Seeds

GARDEN OF DISCOVERY

Everybody knows that Columbus discovered America, but few realize that he also began an exchange of **seeds** between the continents, changing the old and new worlds forever. The kit contains six packets of varieties involved in the seed exchange: seeds that came to the old world from the new (marigolds, zinnias, sunflowers, and zucchini); and seeds that came to the new world from the old (lettuce and daisies). Planting instructions, gardening tips, and activity sheets are included.

Send: $1.75 postage & handling

Ask For: Discover Seeds kit

Mail To: Discover Seeds
P.O. Box 727
Hatboro, PA 19040

Dog or Cat Art Stamp & Catalog

IMPRESS PET OWNERS

Like their pets, dog and cat owners are unique breeds. Identify yourself as a pet lover with a **rubber stamp** impression on your next letter. This one-inch square stamp features a drawing of a happy cat or dog holding a leash in its mouth. The rubber stamp, which is valued at $4.50, also comes with a catalog of hundreds of other stamps.

Send: $2.00 postage & handling

Ask For: Dog or cat art stamp & catalog

Mail To: The Stamp Pad Company, Inc.
P.O. Box 43
Dept. FP
Big Lake, MN 55309

Cookie Cutter

MAKE NO BONES ABOUT IT

This **bone-shaped cookie cutter and the tasty recipe for Cheddar Cheese Dog Biscuits** will have your pooch eating out of your hand. Dogs love cheese, and this recipe also includes healthy wheat flour and wheat germ.

When you've finished making dog biscuits, you can pull out your favorite sugar cookie recipe and use the bone-shaped cutter to make some amusing cookies for humans.

Send: $2.00 postage & handling

Ask For: Bone-shaped cookie cutter & dog biscuit recipe

Mail To: Gifts by Gwen
4212 Thomas Street
Oceanside, CA 92056

• • • • • • • • • • • • • • • • • •

Dorm Checklist

EDUCATIONAL ESSENTIALS

Off to college? Before you fill your dad's station wagon, be sure to study this helpful **Dorm Essentials Checklist.** The 8-1/2" x 11" sheet educates you about the kinds of needs you might have and lists items you might otherwise leave buried at home, such as a flashlight, wastebasket, and tool kit.

Send: A long SASE

Ask For: Dorm Essentials checklist

Mail To: The Complete Traveler
490 Route 46 East
Fairfield, NJ 07004

• • • • • • • • • • • • • • • • • •

Fishing Aid

PIG ON A JIG

Want to see fish act like pigs? Just slip a Dri Rind® trailer onto your jig and watch the fish go hog wild. Dri Rind is a biodegradable sheepskin trailer that gives fishermen great swimming action without the mess of pork rind solutions.

Dri Rind is specially treated and printed in vivid colors that attract fish. And when it absorbs water, it swells up to provide a thicker, meatier, and more naturally flowing attraction that gets them biting. Send for a **Pro Test Pack of Dri Rind** containing two trailers and get some soo-weet action.

Send: $1.00 postage & handling

Ask For: Pro Test Pack of Dri Rind trailers

Mail To: Fred Arbogast Company
313 West North Street
Akron, OH 44303

Ranch Directory

HEY, DUDE

Saddle up for a foot-stompin' good time at a western dude ranch. Lasso this **Old West Dude Ranch Vacations** directory; read all about more than 50 rootin', tootin' ranches; and then decide just which exciting packaged vacation suits your family.

American Wilderness Experience, publisher of the 24-page guide, offers America's oldest and largest ranch selection and reservation service.

Send: Your name & address

Ask For: Old West Dude Ranch Vacations directory

Mail To: Old West Dude Ranch Vacations
P.O. Box 1486   Or call toll-free:
Boulder, CO 80306   1-800-444-DUDE

Brochure & Coupon

ORGANICALLY GROWN INFANTS

According to experts, the overuse of synthetic pesticides in agriculture will soon prove quite dangerous to our children. That's why many parents choose to feed their children certified organically grown foods like those used in Earth's Best Baby Food.

To find out more about natural baby food, request the six-panel *Earth's Best Baby Food* **brochure and coupon** for a free jar or bottle when you buy four.

Send: A long SASE

Ask For: *Earth's Best Organic Baby Food* brochure & coupon

Mail To: Earth's Best Freebie Offer
P.O. Box 887
Middlebury, VT 05753

••••••••••••••••

Eight Baglets

TAG YOUR BAGS

That's right . . . tag your **eight baglets for potpourri or tea** and give them as personalized gifts to your discriminating friends.

This unique kit, which lets you package your own flower or tea blends, comes with complete instructions for filling and sealing the filter-type bags, which measure about 2-1/2" square.

Send: $1.00 postage & handling

Ask For: Eight baglets for potpourri or tea

Mail To: Woolie Works—Baglets
6201 East Huffman Road
Anchorage, AK 99516

••••••••••••••••

Bookmark Kit

ELEPHANT TASK

Who better than an elephant to remind you where you left off reading? It has a great memory and will work for peanuts.

When completed, this needlepoint **elephant bookmark kit** features a cute little elephant character to flag your spot in a book. Squeeze its cheeks and its trunk opens with enough room to stash a small candy inside. The kit includes directions, plastic canvas, yarn, and notions.

Send: $1.75 postage & handling

Ask For: Elephant bookmark kit

Mail To: K & K Marketing
16 Baker Street— Waldron Acres
Kankakee, IL 60901-5900

•••••••••••••••••••

10 Rock
Maple Rings

A CRAFTY OFFER

Those with a knack for arts and crafts can turn this pack of 10 circular **maple wood rings** into everything from napkin rings to toy jewelry for kids. All rings are unfinished and smooth, although some are polished. They are 1-3/4" in diameter and 1/2" thick.

Send: $2.00 postage & handling

Ask For: 10 rock maple rings

Mail To: Elwood Turner Company
HCR Box 132
Morrisville, VT 05661

•••••••••••••••••••

Bumper Sticker

ELTON JOHN BY REQUEST

East End Lights, the international magazine for fans of Elton John, is offering a free **Elton John bumper sticker.** The sticker measures 3" x 11-1/2" and prominently displays "Elton" in bold blue uppercase letters on a yellow background.

A sample copy of *East End Lights* is also available for just $2.00 (a $5.00 value). The slick, collectible publication is filled with news and features about Elton penned by top rock-music journalists.

Send: A long SASE

Ask For: Elton John bumper sticker

Mail To: *East End Lights*
Dept. FB
P.O. Box 760
New Baltimore, MI 48047

Memorabilia

ELVIS WAS HERE

Have you seen Elvis? Elvis sightings have almost become a national pastime. This **joke certificate and pen set** states that you actually have seen the King. The certificate is suitable for framing and is printed on fine parchment paper. And it comes with a ballpoint pen that has I SAW ELVIS, TOO printed on it.

Send: $1.50 postage & handling

Ask For: I Saw Elvis certificate & pen set

Mail To: MailAway USA
635 North Milpas Street
Santa Barbara, CA 93103

Emergency Stickers

FAST FINGERS

When you see an emergency, your fingers have to fly, and you've got to phone for help immediately. However, in a crisis, it's easy to forget the phone numbers you need. That's why you need to place these **four bright emergency phone stickers** on or near your home's phones. That way you'll remember exactly what your fingers need to do.

Send: $1.00 postage & handling

Ask For: Four emergency phone stickers

Mail To: S. Brown
P.O. Box 568
Techny, IL 60082

••••••••••••••••••

Endometriosis
pamphlet

END THE
PAIN

An estimated four to six million American women of reproductive age suffer from a disease called endometriosis, which may cause infertility. However, because it is often difficult to diagnose, many never realize they have it, and suffer the painful symptoms needlessly. Call for a **free pamphlet on endometriosis** explaining the symptoms, causes, and treatments for the disease.

Call Toll-Free: 1-800-221-5005

Ask For: Endometriosis pamphlet

••••••••••••••••••

Ornaments

WARM &
WONDERFUL

Anyone familiar with Mary Engelbreit's warm and witty illustrations will want to own a sleigh-full of these **Mary Engelbreit Gift Collection ornaments.** Anyone who has not yet met Engelbreit's imaginative art (available widely on greeting cards) can sample her creativity by requesting one of the colorful Christmas decorations.

The sturdy, pressed-board ornaments bear glossy Christmas illustrations on both sides and measure about 4" x 5" each.

Send: $2.00 postage & handling for each

Ask For: Mary Engelbreit Gift Collection ornament

Mail To: Sav-on
Dept. O
P.O. Box 1356
Gwinn, MI 49841

Entertainment
Booklet

No Baby Blues

Do you have a bored baby? A "terrible" two-year-old who needs diversion? Then you need this helpful 16-page activity booklet called *100 Ways to Entertain Your Baby.*

Written by an educational media specialist, the straightforward booklet lists simple, age-appropriate activities for grown-ups to do with children ages three and under.

Send: $1.00 postage & handling

Ask For: *100 Ways to Entertain Your Baby* activity Booklet

Mail To: Dr. Nancy Everhart
221 Catawissa Street
Tamaqua, PA 18252

Entertaining-at-
Home Guide

Throw the Perfect Party

Few know more about putting guests in a good mood than the people at Jim Beam. The makers of one of America's favorite bourbons have put together a **16-page guide** on entertaining at home. Filled with helpful hints and original recipes, the full-color guide is a must for all serious party planners.

Send: Your name & address

Ask For: *Entertaining at Home: An American Basic*

Mail To: *Entertaining at Home: An American Basic*
c/o Jim Beam Public Relations Dept. (FR)
510 Lake Cook Road
Deerfield, IL 60015

Christmas Stickers

'TIS THE SEASON

Here are some Christmas decorations that can go anywhere. These **11 silk-screened stickers** are all different and all colorful. They are two inches square with a unique design screened onto a silver background. The stickers include Santa Claus, a Christmas tree, a gingerbread man, and many others. Stick them on cards, notes, or invitations to your Christmas party.

Send: $1.00 postage & handling

Ask For: 11 Christmas stickers

Mail To: Expressions
1668 Valtec Lane
Dept. CFB
Boulder, CO 80301

Electrical Outlet Caps

A SHOCKING COVER-UP

If you're a concerned parent, the last thing you want to see is your young child playing near electrical outlets. The best way to eliminate any chance of accidental shocks is to cover unused outlets with plastic caps. For a modest fee you'll receive **20 sturdy plastic electrical outlet caps,** enough to defuse all potential problem areas in your home.

Send: $2.00 postage & handling

Ask For: 20 electrical outlet caps

Mail To: F & H Baby Products
P.O. Box 566-F
Chagrin Falls, OH 44022

• • • • • • • • • • • • • • • • •

Bird Report

FEATHERED FRIENDS

Find out what your particular type of bird needs to stay happy, healthy, and safe. This two- to four-page **report** produced by a bird breeder explains the best place for your bird's cage, how to tell when the bird is sick, and even the type of toys to buy.

Send: $1.00 & a long SASE

Ask For: Tips about birds

Mail To: J.T.
P.O. Box 5833
Parsippany, NJ 07054

• • • • • • • • • • • • • • • • •

U.S. Money
Information
Booklet

MONEY TALK

Whether you collect coins or just like money, you're likely to find something of interest in this **Federal Reserve pamphlet** on United States currency. There is information on how coins and bills are designed, how U.S. currency is circulated, and the story behind that mysterious Great Seal of the United States. Also included is a brochure on how to identify counterfeit bills.

Send: Your name & address

Ask For: *Fundamental Facts About U.S. Money*

Mail To: The Federal Reserve Bank of Atlanta
Public Affairs Dept.
104 Marietta St., NW
Atlanta, GA 30303-2713

• • • • • • • • • • • • • • • • • •

Pet Literature

HUMANE EDUCATION

Educate yourself and your family about the plight of homeless animals, and learn how you can be a responsible pet owner. Read **Feline and Canine Times**, a publication that focuses on the welfare of cats and dogs.

Produced by Feline & Canine Friends, a nonprofit corporation, the 14-page newsletter includes informative articles and first-aid advice.

Send: A long SASE with 58 cents in postage affixed

Ask For: *Feline and Canine Times*

Mail To: Feline & Canine Friends, Inc.
505 N. Bush Street
Anaheim, CA 92805

• • • • • • • • • • • • • • • • • •

Fig Leaflets

THE FITNESS FRUIT

High in fiber but low in fat, dried figs make exceptionally delightful, nutritious snacks or additions to spreads, salads, and baked goods.

Learn more about these amazingly healthful fruits by sending for the three leaflets titled **Fabulous Figs, the Fitness Fruit; New Buyer's Guide to Dietary Fiber;** and **This Fig Can Teach You a Lot About Nutrition.**

Send: A long SASE

Ask For: Three leaflets: *Fabulous Figs;*
New Buyer's Guide; and
This Fig Can Teach You a Lot About Nutrition

Mail To: California Fig Advisory Board
Dept. F
P.O. Box 709
Fresno, CA 93712

• • • • • • • • • • • • • • • •
Catalog & Guide
FISH
WISHERY

If you're a fishing fan, you'll want a copy of the famous **Mepps Fishing Guide,** a fishing "wish book" that supplies lures as well as information on how to use spinners and spoons.

Sheldons', publisher of the 48-page catalog, also sponsors angler awards and special contests for kids. Its guide includes interesting feature articles and color photos contributed by readers.

Send: Your name & address

Ask For: *Mepps Fishing Guide*

Mail To: Mepps-Sheldon's, Inc.
626 Center Street
Dept. 186
Antigo, WI 54409-2496

• • • • • • • • • • • • • • • •
Flea Control Info
COMB
TOGETHER

You probably don't like to think about all the chemicals in the sprays, powders, and collars you use to control fleas on your pet. Well, now you can combat fleas instantly with an ingenious comb that catches them as you groom your pet.

So spend some time with your cat or dog and be kind to the environment, too. Find out more about the Fleamaster® Flea Comb by requesting **information on flea control without pesticides.**

Send: Your name & address

Ask For: Information on flea control without pesticides

Mail To: Breeders Equipment Co.
Box 177
Flourtown, PA 19031

Kids & Drinking

FLOWING CONVERSATION

Don't keep your thoughts and feelings about alcohol and your kids bottled up. *Let's Talk About Drinking: A Guide for Families* is a **22-page booklet** for discussion between parents and adolescents about underage drinking. It has already proven to be of great benefit to tens of thousands of families.

Send: Your name & address

Ask for: *Let's Talk About Drinking: A Guide for Families*

Mail To: Let's Talk
WSWA
1023 15th Street, NW, Suite 400
Washington, DC 20005-2602

Fruit & Vegetable Recipe Brochures

EATING RIGHT

It's no secret that one key to good health is to cut out sweets and fats in favor of fruits and vegetables. But turning those fruits and vegetables into tasty dishes can be a problem.

This collection of **four full-color recipe books** will give you new ideas on how to prepare healthy entrées and side dishes. You'll learn about cooking stir-fry in the microwave or whipping up passion fruit daiquiris.

Send: $2.00 and a long SASE

Ask For: *Exotic Fruits, Squash Lover's Guide, Frieda's Favorites,* and *Microweavable Guide*

Mail To: Frieda's, Inc.
P.O. Box 58488-FB
Los Angeles, CA 90058

• • • • • • • • • • • • • • • •

Cat Lovers
Cat-Alog
FELINE
FANATICS

Most cat owners are anything but casual in their regard for their feline friends. Now you can order everything from sweatshirts to stationery with clever cat designs. Simply send off for this *Cat Lovers Cat-Alog* and, as a special bonus, you'll receive six cat-design **stickers.** For those who love cats, this may be a purrfect offer.

Send:	$1.00 postage & handling
Ask For:	*Cat Lovers Cat-Alog* and six cat stickers
Mail To:	Gabby Tabby
	Attention: Freebies Offer
	79 A Columbia Avenue
	Cedarhurst, NY 11516

• • • • • • • • • • • • • • • •

Food Supplement
GAS
SHORTAGE

Thanks to Beano™, a new **natural food supplement,** you can now enjoy foods like beans, broccoli, cabbage and whole-grain cereals and breads without the gas. Just three to eight drops of Beano in a single serving are enough to neutralize the complex sugars that cause gas. Request your free 12-serving sample today.

Phone:	1-800-257-8650 (weekdays, 8:30 A.M. to 5:30 P.M. EST)
Ask For:	Beano sample
Limit:	One per household

Multi-use Key Ring

HOP TO IT

You better jump on this deal while it's available. It's the **Gas Hopper® 5-in-1 tool.** Made of hardened spring steel, it's a key ring, screwdriver, can opener, bottle opener, and gas-nozzle handle holder. All of the features are useful, but we found the nozzle holder especially handy. Use it to do hands-free fillups at the pump.

Send: $1.75 postage & handling

Ask For: Gashopper key ring

Mail To: Special Products, Dept. F
P.O. Box 6605
Delray Beach, FL 33484

Wellness Pamphlets

IN THE BALANCE

Your life hangs in the balance when you fail to maintain a healthy lifestyle and diet. According to these three information-packed flyers, "healthy eating habits are based on the principles of balance, moderation, and variety."

If you're looking to scale down your fat intake and balance your eating habits, be sure to request *The Diet Balancing Act; Your Wellness Guide;* and *Trim the Fat & Cut Blood Cholesterol for Life.*

Send: $1.00 postage & handling

Ask For: *The Diet Balancing Act;*
Your Wellness Guide; and *Trim the Fat*

Mail To: Wellness Guide
Georgia Egg Commission
Atlanta State Farmers' Market
16 Forest Parkway
Forest Park, GA 30050

Glow Stickers

GLOW FOR IT

We give this offer a glowing review. This package of **27 Glow Stars™ glow-in-the-dark stickers** has a multitude of fun and educational applications.

The package you will receive will have the stars of the heavens as well as the Earth, the Moon, and Saturn. There will also be several smaller circles that can be distant planets or meteors. You will have everything you need to teach a mini-astronomy course.

Send: $1.00 postage & handling

Ask For: Glow Stars™ Mini Kit

Mail To: M. Wormser
               25606 South Ribbonwood Drive
               Sun Lakes, AZ 85248

Glue Gun Projects

STICKY SHOTS

Glue guns make sticky craft projects simple; they help you to complete all kinds of professional-looking projects, including those featured in this 10-panel **glue gun project booklet.**

Spotlighting the Crafty Magic Melt glue gun, this full-color booklet shows you how to make Halloween masks, silk bridal bouquets, fancy barrettes, and more.

Send: A long SASE

Ask For: Glue gun project booklet

Mail To: Adhesive Technologies
               Terri Russell
               Dept. FREEB
               3 Merrill Industrial Drive
               Hampton, NH 13842-1913

• • • • • • • • • • • • • • • •

Gold-Plated Earring Wires with Stones

BARGAIN BAUBLES

You don't need to sacrifice style because of a tight budget. Add to your jewelry box with **two pairs of gold-plated earring wires,** accented with stone drops in assorted shapes and colors. Even better, you'll be helping the American economy, as these products are proudly made in the USA.

Send:	$2.00 postage & handling
Ask For:	Two pairs of gold-plated earring wires with stones
Mail To:	Rita Salvador Dept. EW P.O. Box 1887 Carmichael, CA 95609

• • • • • • • • • • • • • •

Golf Art Stamp & Catalog

SOMETHING FOR DUFFERS

If there's anyone left who doesn't know you're a golfer, you might want to order this **rubber stamp** to mark your personal messages and envelopes. Along with this golf ball–designed rubber stamp, you'll receive a catalog of many others that may be of interest to you and your family. These rubber stamps normally retail for $4.50.

Send:	$2.00 postage & handling
Ask For:	Golf art Stamp & catalog
Mail To:	The Stamp Pad Co., Inc. P.O. Box 43, Dept. FSR Big Lake, MN 55309

Apricot Recipes

GOOD & SWEET

Good, quick food that's made at home is what this booklet titled **Simply Sensational California Apricots** is all about. The 28 different recipes include everything from exotic apricot chicken to apricot pumpkin muffins. You are also provided with nutritional information as well as ways to cook with canned and dried apricots.

Send: A long SASE

Ask For: *Simply Sensational* booklet

Mail To: California Apricot Advisory Board
1280 Boulevard Way,
Dept. FB
Walnut Creek, CA 94595

Pamphlet

GOOD SPORTS

Injuries to children are commonplace—each year, more than 170,000 children are hurt on playgrounds, more than 500,000 children are hurt on bicycles, and over 2,000 children die in pool-related accidents. This pamphlet, titled **Good Sports: Tips for Making Kids' Recreation Fun and Injury Free,** gives tips on how you can prevent some of these accidents with simple steps. When it comes to your children, it is definitely better to be safe than sorry.

Send: A long SASE

Ask For: *Good Sports* pamphlet

Mail To: The Association of Trial Lawyers of America (ATLA)
Dept. FRG
P.O. Box 3744
Washington, DC 20007-0244

Growth Chart

POPPING UP

"My, how they've grown" is the exclamation from Grandma every time she stops in for a visit. Now you can show her just exactly how much the kids have popped up with this colorful 8" x 41" polyethylene **child's growth chart** from Jolly Time Popcorn. Parents can mark important dates on the hanging chart to create a lasting record of growth up to five feet tall.

Send: Five proofs of purchase from Jolly Time products or $1.00 plus two proofs of purchase

Ask For: Child's growth chart plus Jolly Time coupon

Mail To: Jolly Time Popcorn Growth Chart
P.O. Box 178
Dept. FB
Sioux City, IA 51102

Color Catalog of Earrings

A PIERCING PROBLEM

Pierced earrings are certainly stylish, but some people find that clipping metal ornaments to their lobes results in an allergic reaction.

That no longer needs to be a problem once you order this **catalog of hypoallergenic earrings** and jewelry. Included with the eight-page color catalog is a **coupon for a free pair** of earrings that can be redeemed with your first order.

Send: $1.00 postage & handling

Ask For: Hypoallergenic earring catalog and coupon

Mail To: H & A Enterprises, Inc.
143-19 25th Avenue
P.O. Box 489F
Whitestone, NY 11357

Costume Booklet

SPOOKED NO MORE

Halloween can be pretty spooky for parents. Somehow October 31 creeps up too quickly, and grown-ups get caught without the necessary witch and goblin outfits for their trick-or-treaters.

That's why this handy booklet called *Fast & Easy Halloween Costumes for Kids* will prove a real treat for adults looking for no-sew, low-cost, last-minute costumes. On its pages the desperate—and the prepared—will find illustrated instructions for 20 original, humorous costumes.

Send: $2.00 postage & handling

Ask For: *Fast & Easy Halloween Costumes for Kids*

Mail To: Alpel Publishing
P.O. Box 203—FBH
Chambly PQ J3L 4B3
Canada   (Postage to Canada is 40¢)

Porcelain Doll Dress Pattern

DRESS UP YOUR DOLL

Maybe you collect porcelain baby dolls but have no idea where to get new outfits for them. Instead of endless searching, sew your own. You can do this with the help of a special porcelain **doll clothes pattern** for a christening dress, bonnet, and panties. This pattern fits a ten-inch, soft-body doll. You can also request a catalog for an additional fee.

Send: 29-cent stamp and/or $2.00 for catalog

Ask For: Porcelain-doll dress pattern

Mail To: Handmade by Peg®
P.O. Box 514 FR
Gales Ferry, CT 06335

• • • • • • • • • • • • • • •

Allergy and Pet
Booklet

No-Sneeze Kitty

If someone in your family is allergic to cats, it often means that kitty will be finding a new home or must live outside. New information is now available that can help. *How to Allergy-Proof Your Pet* is an informative booklet that shows you how to take several easy steps that can ease the sneeze and keep kitty in the house. How to curb kitty's dander, the primary cause of allergic reactions, is one of the topics addressed in this booklet. Other helpful tips on desensitizing your house are also included.

Send: $1.00 postage & handling

Ask For: *How to Allergy-Proof Your Pet*

Mail to: Associated Humane Societies
124 Evergreen, Dept. F
Newark, NJ 07114

• • • • • • • • • • • • • • •

Rawhide Pet Bone

Rowdy Yates Was Here

Rawhide was a great TV show and Beef rawhide is the ingredient in this **seven-inch white rawhide bone** for your bowser. This great treat can satisfy your dog's chewing urges and help promote healthy teeth and gums. It is oven-cured and is a natural approach to nutrition. This all-beef rawhide bone is a tasty way to make man's best friend happy and may save your favorite pair of slippers.

Send: $1.50 postage & handling

Ask For: seven-inch white rawhide bone

Mail To: Prime Pet Products
P.O. Box 2473
Beverly Hills, CA 90212

• • • • • • • • • • • • • • • •
Sing-along Songs
ROCK-A-BYE-BABY

"Hush little baby, don't say a word, Mama's going to buy you a mockingbird" are the lead words in one of the 22 favorite **sing-along songs** for babies in this adorable purse-size 32-page book. It's fun to look at and fun to sing to your little ones. All the words to all of your favorites are included.

Send:	$1.00 postage & handling plus a long SASE with two first-class stamps affixed
Ask For:	Lullaby songs for babies
Mail To:	Practical Parenting Lullaby Songs 18326 Minnetonka Boulevard Dept. LULL-FRBE Deephaven, MN 55391

• • • • • • • • • • • • • • • •
Football Mini-Book
NOT FOR WOMEN ONLY

A strange phenomenon occurs every fall, when millions of viewers become stuck to their television on weekends and Monday evenings. What causes this stickiness?? It's football, arguably America's favorite sport. Unfortunately, not everyone who watches football understands what's going on. The **48-page minibook** *A Woman's Guide to Football* helps clear the mystery. It's easy to read and guides anyone (not just women) through the basics to strategy. Send for this book and score points!

Send:	$2.00 postage & handling
Ask For:	Football guide
Mail To:	Schultz Communications 9412 Admiral Nimitz, NE Albuquerque, NM 87111

Catnip Toy

CAT-FISH-NIP

The purrfect gift for any cat is this all-natural catnip fish. Constructed from 100% cotton denim and adorned with decorative stitching and a button eye, this **catnip fish** is filled with organically grown catnip and flowers—absolutely no pesticides are used. It is not sealed in plastic, so the full bouquet and aroma of the catnip can be enjoyed by your cat. Available in yellow, fuchsia, or teal. This catnip fish usually sells for $4.95 plus $2.00 postage and handling, but it is yours for only $2.00.

Send: $2.00 postage & handling

Ask For: Cat-fish (specify color of your choice)

Mail To: Cat-fish
3680 Keir Lane
Helena, MT 59601-9722

Limit: One per name or address

Christmas Pet Stocking Pattern

NO-RUN STOCKINGS

If your pet is like one of the family then it needs a Christmas stocking to hang on the mantle with the others. Complete instructions come with this **pattern** along with helpful hints on decorating the pet paw stocking to match your pet's personality. Sew this easy-to-make pattern by hand or machine. What family pet wouldn't appreciate a handmade gift?

Send: $1.00 postage & handling

Ask For: Pet paw pattern

Mail to: Raveled Yarns
P.O. Box 1953
South Bend, IN 46634-1953

• • • • • • • • • • • • • • • • • •

Booklet and Map

ALL IN FREE!

Find your way through the wilderness without road signs by using your compass and the knowledge that you gleaned from this **sample orienteering map and ten-page booklet.** Orienteering is the art of finding your way through the wilderness using only a compass and a map to plan your route. You get the booklet, a sample map, and a listing of orienteering clubs.

Send: A long SASE

Ask For: Orienteering map and booklet

Mail To: Silva Orienteering Services
Dept. FBS
P.O. Box 1604
Binghamton, NY 13902

• • • • • • • • • • • • • • • • • •

Booklet

BASKETBALL JONES WAS HERE

Slam dunk your way through history with this informative **booklet about the history of basketball.** Did you know that basketball was developed in the United States? Or that it began with a peach basket for a hoop? Learn this and other exciting facts in this booklet titled *Basketball Was Born Here.* You'll also get a color brochure about the Basketball Hall of Fame located in Springfield, Massachusetts, the home of basketball.

Send: $1.00 and a long SASE

Ask For: *Basketball Was Born Here* booklet

Mail To: Basketball Hall of Fame
1150 West Columbus Avenue
Springfield, MA 01101

• • • • • • • • • • • • • • • •

Bumper Sticker

STICK TO THIS

If you want to let others know about your fondness for felines, then you need a **Home Is Where Your Cat Is bumper sticker** for your car. Stick one on the car, the RV, or the dog house next door. The bumper stickers come in assorted colors and are a perfect way to express your opinion about your favorite pet.

Send: $1.00 postage & handling

Ask For: Purrfect bumper sticker

Mail To: Pet Pride
P.O. Box 1055
Pacific Palisades, CA 90272

• • • • • • • • • • • • • • • •

Pet Treats

A SNAPPY IDEA

You can spoil your dog or cat and not worry about its health when you give it a treat filled with natural vitamins and minerals. **Cat Snap Treats and Dog Snap Treats** are tasty morsels that your pet will find hard to resist. These tasty treats also help promote a healthy and glossy coat. Plus, it's a great way to reward your pet.

Send: $2.00 postage & handling

Ask For: Cat or dog snap sample

Mail To: Prime Pet Products
P.O. Box 2473
Beverly Hills, CA 90212

Flyer

HORSESHOE RULES

If you think horseshoes belong only on horses' hooves, then you're missing out on a terrific old game in which people toss horseshoes at metal stakes. The game of horseshoes will help you develop your body coordination and aim, and it's fun to play at picnics and barbecues.

Interested? Then send for this eight-panel flyer of **horseshoe pitching rules** from the National Horseshoe Pitchers' Association. It explains the ins and outs of court layout and horseshoe competition.

Send: A long SASE

Ask For: Horseshoe pitching rules

Mail To: NHPA
Box 7927
Columbus, OH 43207

Motel Directory

HOST OF COUPONS

Budget Host Inns, an economy chain of U.S. and Canadian motels, will gladly send you its *Budget Host Travel Directory*, which features Bottom-Line Bonus Coupons for extra savings beyond the network's economy rates. The chain has a toll-free reservations number that connects you directly to the front desk of the inn you choose.

Send: Your name & address

Ask For: *Budget Host Travel Directory*

Mail To: Budget Host Inns
P.O. Box 10656
Ft. Worth, TX 76114

Warning Flyers

No Hot Dogs

•••••••••••••••••••••

Have you ever noticed a dog panting miserably in a hot car? Now you can do something to help him.

Carry this set of **five Hot Car flyers** titled *Your Dog May Be Dying*, and place one under the hot car's windshield wiper.

Prepared by the Animal Protection Institute of America, each bright red flyer carries a detailed warning about the dangers that hot cars pose to dogs.

Send:	A long SASE
Ask For:	Set of five Hot Car *(Your Dog May Be Dying)* flyers
Mail To:	Freebie HCF Offer P.O. Box 22505 Sacramento, CA 95822

ID Bracelets

Who Am I?

•••••••••••••••••••••

If you're in a large crowd, on a family vacation, or just shopping in the mall with your children, there is always the chance that the kids may wander off. You can help protect your child with an I.D. Me **identification wristband.** The wristbands are waterproof and the low price makes them disposable. They're simple to use: just write the ID information on the underside of the band in pen and place it on your child's wrist.

Send:	$1.00 and a long SASE
Ask For:	Two ID Me™ Wristbands
Mail To:	Practical Parenting 18326 Minnetonka Boulevard Dept. ID-FRBE Deephaven, MN 55391

• • • • • • • • • • • • • • • •

Name Tag

IDENTIFY YOURSELF

Look official: order a 1" x 3" plastic **name tag** engraved with the name or number of your choice. Specify up to 24 letters and select a blue, red, or black tag with white letters, or a white tag with black letters, that will attach easily to your key chain or luggage. You may order as many as you like.

Send: $1.25 for each tag
(please print names or numbers clearly)

Ask For: Name or number tag

Mail To: Jansco
P.O. Box 6062
Dept. S
Chillicothe, OH 45601

• • • • • • • • • • • • • • • •

Jewelry Instructions

ART-TO-WEAR

Titled *Jewelry by You,* this ten-page instructional booklet provides superb ideas and directions for creating original earrings and pins from materials you'll find at craft stores. You start with ivory-colored mat board and embellish it with acrylic paints, beads, rhinestones, and sequins. An excellent value, the 8-1/2" x 11" booklet also includes full-size patterns for each project.

Send: $1.00 postage & handling

Ask For: *Jewelry by You*

Mail To: Pegasus Originals, Inc.
Dept. 170
129 Minnie Fallaw Road
Lexington, SC 29073

Travel Aid

DRY DUDS

Use your portable hair dryer to dry your clothes whenever you travel—or when you simply can't wait for that favorite swimsuit or pair of shorts to air-dry. How? Simply pull out this ingenious **Jiffy Dryer**, insert your hair dryer and watch it dry small garments in minutes.

The 6" x 23", fire-retardant, reusable bag has glue strips at one end and vents at the other, and it measures just 2-1/4" x 6" when folded flat.

Send: $1.75 postage & handling

Ask For: Jiffy Dryer

Mail To: The Complete Collegiate
490 Route 46 East
Fairfield, NJ 07004

Popcorn ball maker

HAVE A BALL

Looking for fun? Jolly Time® Popcorn is offering a clever gadget that helps turn plain popcorn into irresistible confections. It's a durable, two-piece, plastic **popcorn ball maker** that creates perfect 3-1/2" popcorn balls every time without ever getting your fingers sticky or burned. Also included are two popular recipes for popcorn balls.

Send: $1.00 postage & handling for one, $1.75 for two

Ask For: Jolly Time popcorn ball maker

Mail To: Jolly Time Popcorn
P.O. Box 178
Dept. FBB
Sioux City, IA 51102

• • • • • • • • • • • • • • • • •

Nurse Humor Magazine Sample Copy

HOSPITAL HILARITY

Now we know how nurses are able to care for the ill and still manage a friendly smile. The **Journal of Nursing Jocularity** is a humor magazine devoted to the lighter side of health care. The articles, puzzles, and jokes are all aimed at the funny bone. And the fact that *Library Journal* selected this as one of the 10 Best magazines of 1991 is no laughing matter.

Send: $2.00 postage & handling

Ask For: Sample copy of the *Journal of Nursing Jocularity*

Mail To: JNJ–Freebies
P.O. Box 40416
Mesa, AZ 85274

• • • • • • • • • • • • • • • •

Pregnancy Book

BIRTH MIRTH

What can you expect when you're expecting? While no one can fully prepare you for the personal experience of pregnancy, this 96-page **paperback book titled *The Joy of Pregnancy*** addresses a wide range of topics relating to childbirth.

This full-color, generously illustrated book consists of more than 40 sections, each focusing on a different topic, such as nutrition, emotions, and labor. Written in simple terms, it also includes a glossary and an index.

Send: $1.75 postage & handling

Ask For: *The Joy of Pregnancy* book

Mail To: D&S Distributors
P.O. Box 3013
Pocatello, ID 83201

Child Safety Brochures

CERTIFIED SAFE

Parents, grandparents, and child-care providers want babies and toddlers to live safely, so the Juvenile Products Manufacturers Association, (JPMA), which sponsors a product safety certification program, will send concerned adults **two brochures on juvenile safety.**

One eight-panel brochure describes how to determine whether a crib is a safe place for baby, and the eight-page *Be Sure It's Safe!* is a guide for choosing a variety of juvenile products.

Send: A long SASE

Ask For: Crib safety brochure & *Be Sure It's Safe!*

Mail To: JPMA
Two Greentree Centre
Suite 225, Box 955
Marlton, NJ 08053

Kahlua Wedding Cake Card

A CAKE WITH A KICK

Chocolate, granulated sugar, and flour: these are ingredients you'd expect to find in a wedding cake. But if you're looking for something special on your special day, consider adding a few cups of Kahlua mocha-flavored liqueur to the mix.

Send away for this colorful card, which contains **three recipes** for both cakes and frosting.

Send: Your name & address

Ask For: Kahlua wedding cake card

Mail To: Kahlua Wedding Cake Card
Dept. KWC
P.O. Box 2426
Farmington Hills, MI 48333-2426

• • • • • • • • • • • • • • • • •

Pet Brush

KNOTTY PROBLEMS

One thing animals do on a regular basis is get snarls in their hair. They have to rely upon their human friends when their hairs get out of hand.

That's what this handy dandy, brightly colored plastic **pet brush** is for. It'll tame the most terrible tangle and comb out the most cockleburred coat. Choose from red, yellow, white, black, green, or blue.

Send: $1.50 each postage & handling, or $3.00 for three

Ask For: Pet brush (give color choice)

Mail To: Prairie Flower
Pet Brush
P.O. Box 8664
Riverside, CA 92515

• • • • • • • • • • • • • • • • •

Newsletter

WHAT A LAUGH

Dedicated to the healing art of humor, *The Laughter Prescription Newsletter* is a monthly publication that offers jokes and articles on humor and healing.

Send for a copy and learn what patients and hospitals have found: the eight-page newsletter and the laughter it encourages can provide comic relief to those in physical and emotional pain.

Send: $1.25 plus a long SASE with 52 cents postage affixed

Ask For: Sample issue of *The Laughter Prescription Newsletter*

Mail To: *The Laughter Prescription Newsletter*
19300 Rinaldi Street
P.O. Box 7985
Northridge, CA 91327-7985

Stress Booklet

STAY COOL

In today's hectic world no one is free from stress. Learn how to keep your stress level low with this free booklet, *The Less Stress Handbook.* It's easy to read, and the tips on reducing stress are easy to implement. A bibliography for additional reading is also included. By adopting some of the recommended procedures, you can reduce the stress in your life.

Send: Your name & address

Ask For: *The Less Stress Handbook*

Mail To: Stress Relief Institute Free Booklet Offer
Radio City Station
P.O. Box 1095
New York, NY 10101-1095

Food Newsletter

YOU ARE WHAT YOU EAT

Easy, low-fat recipes and sinful desserts are what you get in your free sample issues of *Let's Talk Food*. This **eight-page newsletter** opens with a column from the editor/publisher and follows with easy-to-make recipes that are good to eat and good for you. New food products and related culinary items are also featured. Plus, the editor also realizes that occasionally there is the need for a yummy high-fat rich dessert recipe (low-fat substitutes are also recommended).

Send: Your name & address

Ask For: *Let's Talk Food* newsletter

Mail To: *Let's Talk Food*
47 Lehigh Road
Wellesley, MA 02181

• • • • • • • • • • • • • • • • •

Emergency ID
LIFE ALERT

An emergency medical card or tag can mean the difference between life and death in an accident.

Now you can fit all your medical data—plus thumbprints—on one card or tag. Send for an **order form for Life Alert ID,** complete the data section (which will appear in microfilm form on your card) and then mail just $3.00 for a wallet-size card with photo or $2.50 for a 1-1/2" x 2-1/4" tag.

Send: A long SASE

Ask For: Brochure & order form for the Life Alert ID card and/or tag

Mail To: Life Alert ID
Rt. 2, Box 232
Denton, NC 27239

• • • • • • • • • • • • • • • • •

Sampler Fabric
PICTURE PERFECT

Master a craft that's simple and fun to do; request **fabric printed for a liquid embroidery sampler** and try your hand at applying ballpoint paint, found at crafts stores.

Choose from these designs printed on large pieces of muslin: a detailed 11" x 18" Christmas stocking; an 11-1/2-inch square butterfly with floral border; or a patriotic 5-1/2" x 4" drum complete with eagle.

Send: $2.00 postage & handling

Ask For: Liquid embroidery sampler and print material; specify stocking, butterfly or drum

Mail To: Angel Honey Undt
34 Main Street
P.O. Box 74
Morrisville, VT 05661

Worm Keeper

LIVELY DE-BAIT

The early bird catches the worm it's true, but the fisherman with the late worm catches nothing. Serious fishermen know the importance of keeping bait alive and wiggling. This trial-size pack of **Worm Keeper organic humus** will keep an eight-ounce bait canteen of worms wet, fed, and cool so they'll attract fish.

Send: $1.25 postage & handling

Ask For: Trial-size Worm Keeper organic humus

Mail To: Plantsitter, Inc.
P.O. Box 6512
Boise, ID 83707

Immunization Schedule

LOVE HURTS

Sometimes love hurts, as it does when parents take children to receive immunizations. However, that infrequent bit of pain protects children against some life-threatening diseases, as this brochure explains.

The six-panel brochure includes the American Academy of Pediatrics' **immunization schedule** plus a credit-card-sized Child Vaccination Record Card on which you can write your child's immunization history.

Send: A long SASE

Ask For: AAP's Immunization Schedule & Vaccination Card

Mail To: AAP's Immunization Schedule, Dept. C
American Academy of Pediatrics
P.O. Box 927
Elk Grove, IL 60009-0927

Limit: One per SASE

••••••••••••••••••

Lungs-at-Work Activity Book

NO-SMOKING PRIMER

It's one thing to tell your children not to smoke and another to show them exactly why they should avoid this harmful habit. This **booklet from the American Lung Association** includes a variety of activities and illustrations that will help convince your kids to stay away from cigarettes.

Send: Your name & address

Ask For: No Smoking, Lungs at Work activity book

Mail To: American Lung Association
P.O. Box 596 FB
No. 0840
New York, NY 10116-0596

••••••••••••••••••

Lyme Disease Brochure

SUMMER THREAT

With its mysterious arthritis-like symptoms, Lyme disease, first diagnosed in 1975, has become a serious health concern, particularly in the northeastern U.S. *Lyme Disease: A Summer Threat* is a six-panel brochure that describes the deer ticks that carry this serious infectious disease as well as the symptoms and treatment for what at first appears to be a flulike illness.

Send: Your name & address

Ask For: Educational brochure on Lyme disease

Mail To: ASCP
Communications and Public Relations Dept.
2100 West Harrison Street
Chicago, IL 60612

● ● ● ● ● ● ● ● ● ● ● ● ● ● ● ● ● ●
Cookbook &
Sample

SEASONAL
OFFER

Cook up some Cajun magic with this 48-page **cookbook and sample packet of Chef Paul Prudhomme's Magic Seasoning Blends.™**

The full-color cookbook is filled with some of the famous Cajun chef's most delicious recipes.

Two one-ounce sample packets of Magic Seasoning Blends are also included. The book contains two coupons worth 50 cents each off future Magic buys. You'll also receive a catalog.

Send:　　$2.50 postage & handling
　　　　　　(check or money order only)

Ask For　Magic Seasoning Blends Cookbook,
　　　　　　two one-ounce sample packets and catalog

Mail To:　Magic Seasoning Blends
　　　　　　P.O. Box 23342
　　　　　　Harahan, LA 70183-0342

● ● ● ● ● ● ● ● ● ● ● ● ● ● ● ● ●
Do-It-Yourself
Picture Frames

PICTURE
PERFECT

One short trip to the art supply store or frame shop and you'll realize the value of making your own picture frames at home. With this **guide** for the do-it-yourselfer, you'll find out how to turn standard mouldings into the perfect frames for your photos, paintings, or posters. The information covers everything from matting your pictures to displaying them on your wall.

Send:　　75 cents postage & handling

Ask For:　*How to Make Picture Frames* pamphlet

Mail To:　WMMPA
　　　　　　Dept. FB92
　　　　　　P.O. Box 25278
　　　　　　Portland, OR 97225

•••••••••••••••••
Holiday Menu

EIGHT AT FOUR

Prepare a big holiday feast with a minimum of fuss; request **Maytag's Holiday Menu for Eight** and follow its step-by-step instructions for preparing a 4:00 P.M. meal of roast turkey, stuffing, cornbread, sweet potatoes, vegetables, sauces, and apple mince pie.

The eight-page booklet even includes a shopping list and a precise time sequence for cooking the foods in both conventional and microwave ovens.

Send: 25 cents in coin

Ask For: *Maytag's Holiday Menu for Eight*

Mail To: Maytag Company
One Dependability Square
Dept. FB92
Newton, IA 50208

•••••••••••••••••
Pharmacists' Chart

SWALLOW 'EM WHOLE

Because they struggle to swallow pills whole, some folks crush their medications in order to ingest them. However, as this **MedChart** indicates, many oral medications should not be crushed or they will lose their potency. This two-page list names 200 common medications that need to remain intact.

Send: A long SASE

Ask For: MedChart, a list of 200 medications that should not be crushed

Mail To: Trademark Medical
Dept. MC
1053 Headquarters Park
Fenton, MO 63026

Medical Release Form

PRE-MED

Prompt medical attention in an emergency can make the difference between life and death. But medical personnel need a parent's permission before administering treatment to a minor, so what happens when you're not around to give the go-ahead?

Just fill in the blanks on this **medical treatment release form** to provide ready legal authority to physicians. It also allows you to provide vital information such as blood type and allergies your children may have.

Send: A long SASE

Ask For: Medical release form

Mail To: Medical Emergency—Practical Parenting
18326 Minnetonka Boulevard
Deephaven, MN 55391

Celebrity Addresses

WRITE HERE, RIGHT NOW

Wouldn't you love to write to Macaulay Culkin, Madonna, or Miss Piggy? First you should write to Michael Levine, author of *The Address Book—How to Reach Anyone Who Is Anyone.*

Send a self-addressed stamped envelope and the author will reveal the exclusive mailing **addresses of 20 superstar celebrities,** including the ones mentioned.

Write to these celebrities with your comments. The author assures us these superstars do respond.

Send: A long SASE

Ask For: Addresses of 20 superstar celebrities

Mail To: Michael Levine/The Address Book
8730 Sunset Boulevard, 6th Floor
Los Angeles, CA 90069

• • • • • • • • • • • • • • • •

Miracle Cleaner

You'll Clean Up

When your kitchen cleanser just won't do the job, it's time for Orange-Solv Liquid **Cleaner.** Just mix this sample with some warm water, then spread it on soap film, ink or tar. Give it a minute to work and wipe it off for a spotless finish. Whether in the kitchen, bathroom, or garage, you'll find countless uses for this miracle cleaner. Order a sample and see for yourself.

Send: $2.00 postage & handling

Ask For: Miracle cleaner sample

Mail To: Atlantic Recycled Paper
P.O. Box 39179 F
Baltimore, MD 21212

• • • • • • • • • • • • • • • •

Doll Kit

Mop It Up

We give this **petite mop doll kit** our "wringing" endorsement. Completed, this little cutie stands about a foot tall and wears ribbons in her hair, a bonnet, and an apron.

Any novice crafter can make her since no sewing is involved. The kit includes mop strands, presewn head, fiberfill, fabric, a wood dowel for support, and illustrated instructions for finishing.

Send: $2.00 postage & handling

Ask For: Mop doll kit

Mail To: The Crafter's Cottage
345 South McDowell Boulevard, Suite 314
Petaluma, CA 94954

Contact Lens Offer

LENSES FOR LESS

If you need to replace a pair of contact lenses, send for a **price sheet** from the National Contact Lens Center. The center can duplicate your current lenses for less than you would normally spend, and you will receive lenses from the same manufacturer and laboratory that made your originals. The company also has a toll-free order number.

Send: A long SASE

Ask For: "Contact Lenses at a Discount" price sheet

Mail To: National Contact Lens Center
3527 Bonita Vista Drive
Santa Rosa, CA 95404

Or call: Toll-free: 1-800-326-6352
Local Santa Rosa call: (707)545-6352

Safety Scissors

CUT UPS

Kids often need scissors to cut out pictures from magazines or make crafts projects for school. But with most razor-sharp scissors, magazines aren't always the only thing that gets cut.

Avoid accidents with a pair of **safety scissors** that are perfectly sized for a child's hand.

Send: $2.00 for three

Ask For: Safety scissors

Mail To: Neetstuf
Dept. F2-36
P.O. Box 459
Stone Harbor, NJ 08247

• • • • • • • • • • • • • • • •

Membership Kit

WHOOO IS UP?

If you perk up at midnight, or if you snooze through mornings, request the **Night Owl Network membership kit** and become a moonlighting member of this exclusive nighttime network. Publisher of a quarterly newsletter written by members, the group seeks to "build a bridge of understanding between owls and larks" (daytime people).

You'll receive a membership card, humorous wall certificate, and catalog.

Send: $1.50 postage & handling

Ask For: Night Owl Network membership kit

Mail To: Night Owl Network
3260 Keith Bridge Road, No. 131
Cumming, GA 30130

• • • • • • • • • • • • • • • •

No-Smoking
Coloring Book

A COLORFUL MESSAGE

The medium is the message with this no-smoking **coloring book** from the American Lung Association. While your children color in the drawings, they can't miss the many urgings to stay away from tobacco products. As the booklet states on the back page, smoking is "a matter of life and breath."

Send: Your name & address

Ask For: No-smoking coloring book

Mail To: American Lung Association
P.O. Box 596 FB
No. 0043
New York, NY 10116-0596

• • • • • • • • • • • • • • • •

Pasta Recipes

USE YOUR NOODLE

Make lasagna from start to finish in just 20 minutes. Impossible, you say. What about all those hot, soggy noodles?

Well, arm yourself with **no-boil pasta recipes and information** and a package of DeFino No Boil lasagna noodles. Then layer the dry noodles with your favorite sauce or one you've made with this offer's lasagna and manicotti recipes. Presto! You've got a scrumptious Italian entrée.

Send: Your name & address

Ask For: DeFino No Boil Pasta information & recipes

Mail To: Shade Pasta, Inc.
P.O. Box 645
Fremont, NE 68025

Or call toll-free: 1-800-NO BOIL-1 (1-800-662-6451)

• • • • • • • • • • • • • • • •

Recipe Booklet

OH, OLIVES!

Let's clear up a myth right now. Olives aren't really that fattening. Even the super colossal olive has only 12 calories. So how about giving olives another chance? Take a look at this beautiful **recipe booklet** that shows you how olives can spice up your pasta, grain, and bean dishes.

Send: Your name & address

Ask For: *Pasta, Grains & Beans* recipe booklet

Mail To: California Olive Industry
Dept. 50
P.O. Box 7796
Fresno, CA 93747

● ● ● ● ● ● ● ● ● ● ● ● ● ● ● ● ●

Fishing Lure

FISH A LURE

From the bayou country of Louisiana comes one of the most effective lures ever developed for catching bream, crappie, and other pan fish. This lure is less expensive and easier to use than live worms or crickets, and you can use it over and over to catch buckets of fish.

Dubbed the **Cajun shad lure,** it has split shot molded right to its head. Use it with or without a cork on a light tackle pole or cane.

Send: $1.00 postage & handling for one;
               $2.00 for three

Ask For: Cajun shad fishing lure

Mail To: Ol' John's Lures
               Route 1, Box 323
               Keatchie, LA 71046

● ● ● ● ● ● ● ● ● ● ● ● ● ● ● ● ●

Watersaving

Crystals

THE GARDENER'S HELPER

No matter how diligent you are about watering your plants on a regular basis, there are just times when you're unable to stay on schedule. These nontoxic, **synthetic polymer crystals** are your best insurance for healthy-looking plants. When mixed in with your houseplant or garden soil, the Water Less Crystals will absorb up to 700 times their weight in water. The excess moisture is then released to the plant as needed.

Send: $2.00 postage & handling

Ask For: Water Less Crystals

Mail To: Organic Products
               P.O. Box 6512
               Boise, ID 83707

Passion Flower Seeds & Brochure

FLOWER POWER

Spanish explorers were so taken with the unusual plant they found in South America, they viewed it as an embodiment of their religious beliefs and named it the passion flower.

Today the passion flower is the perfect houseplant for either indoors or outdoors. With a clinging vine, green leaves, and colorful flowers, this is a plant lover's favorite. Send in for this offer and you'll receive a **brochure and some sample seeds.**

Send: $1.00 postage & handling

Ask For: Passion flower seeds & brochure

Mail To: Passion Flower
P.O. Box 3498
San Rafael, CA 94902

Health Record

PASSPORT FOR PARENTS

As your child journeys through life, you'll want to record his or her medical history and immunization record.

Your Child's Passport to Health, a 12-page booklet that resembles an honest-to-goodness passport, will help you do just that. You'll have important health information at hand whether your family roams or stays at home.

Send: $1.00 postage & handling

Ask For: *Your Child's Passport to Health*

Mail To: Your Child's Passport to Health
P.O. Box 14-F
Streamwood, IL 60107

Peanut Recipe Books

NUTS TO YOU

Mix up some chocolate-peanut no-bake cookies or marinate some exotic meat kabobs in a peanut butter–based sauce. Whatever you choose, you'll be eating protein-packed food that even kids find hard to resist.

The 30-page, recipe-packed books *Microwave Magic* and *It's Easy to Be a Gourmet With Peanuts,* published by the Oklahoma Peanut Board, will have you reaching for peanuts and peanut butter for every meal.

Send:	$1.00 postage &.handling for each book
Ask For:	*Microwave Magic* or *It's Easy to Be a Gourmet with Peanuts*
Mail To:	Oklahoma Peanut Board P.O. Box D Madill, OK 73446

Nutritional Additive

PERKY PET

Providing the perfect nutritional balance is a key to making sure your pet has a long and happy life. **OHD concentrate (Organically Helps Digestion)** is a unique blend of natural minerals, vitamins, and amino acids that does just that for animals and birds.

OHD has been scientifically proven in major university studies to improve the health and longevity of animals and birds.

Send:	$1.00 postage & handling for one
Ask For:	OHD concentrate
Mail To:	Organic Products by Plantsitter P.O. Box 6512 Boise, ID 83707

Birthday Report

PERSONAL HISTORY

Would you like to know more about the date on which you were born? Then be sure to send for a **birthday or anniversary report** that details events that took place on that special day and during that particular year. Each sheet is suitable for framing and bears a hand-applied gold seal.

Send: $3.00 per report

Ask For: Birthday or anniversary report
(request any date from 1850 to 1989)

Mail To: CRM Enterprises
P.O. Box 522-B
Syosset, NY 11791

Personalized Patterns Catalog

HOMEMADE WARDROBE

With the high cost of clothing at your favorite shop or store, you've probably given some thought to making your own outfits. But how do you get started?

That process is made easier when you order a **personalized pattern catalog.** The catalog comes with a $5.00 coupon to apply to your first order. When you order a pattern you will get one that fits perfectly because they are made to your own measurements.

Send: A long SASE with 52 cents in postage affixed

Ask For: Personalized pattern catalog

Mail To: Personalized Patterns of America
7267 Mobile Highway
Pensacola, FL 32526

• • • • • • • • • • • • • • • •

Personalized Print

TWICE BLESSED

Bless a friend with an expression of your fondness; request this **personalized 5" x 7" watercolor print** that features a floral frame encircling the words "When I count my blessings I count YOU twice." You supply your friend's name (up to ten letters), which will appear above the saying.

Accompanied by a catalog of pictures to personalize, the print comes matted and shrink-wrapped.

Send: $2.00 postage & handling plus the name you wish to appear on the print (up to ten letters). Please print name clearly.

Ask For: Personalized 5" x 7" watercolor print and a catalog

Mail To: Simply Elegant
P.O. Box 31155
Dept. FB
St. Louis, MO 63131

• • • • • • • • • • • • • • • •

Pet Owners' Publication

PET GAZETTE

Few people are more passionate than pet owners. Get them started and they eloquently expound on the many virtues of raising and caring for pets.

Pet owners can now enjoy articles, poems and photos submitted by their brethren to the *Pet Gazette.* Send in to receive a sample copy of this 23-page publication.

Send: $2.00 postage & handling

Ask For: *Pet Gazette* sample copy

Mail To: The Pet Gazette
1309 North Halifax
Daytona Beach, FL 32118

Pet Placemat

CUTE
& CLEAN

Your Fido or Tabby makes a mighty mess when he eats from his pet bowl, and you end up using lots of paper towels or newspapers to keep your floor clean.

Why not give your favorite pooch or kitty a **reusable pet placemat** instead? School kids helped to recycle old magazine photos of animals and make them into these laminated, 8" x 10" placemats that invite pets to partake and you simply to wipe up the mess after each meal.

Send:	$2.00 postage & handling
Ask For:	Reusable pet placemat (specify type of pet)
Mail To:	United Earth Friends™ P.O. Box 51106 Raleigh, NC 27609

Photo Cards

PHOTO
GRASP

Why bury your favorite wallet photos in your wallet? Instead, proudly display the darling images of your darlings by attaching these **two magnetic photo cards** to the backs of two favorite photographs.

Simply peel the backing from the adhesive, 2-1/2" x 3-1/2" magnets, place the photos on the flexible magnets and then exhibit your pictures prominently on a refrigerator door or a filing cabinet.

Send:	$2.00 postage & handling
Ask For:	Two magnetic photo cards
Mail To:	Enjoyment Enterprises Dept. PC P.O. Box 1887 Carmichael, CA 95609-1887

Plastic Bag Carriers

GRAB BAGS

Does carrying plastic grocery bags cut off the circulation in your hands? Pinch your fingers? Then pick up a **pair of Finger Savers.** A unique new invention, these molded plastic bag carriers feature a hook for handling multiple bags and provide a wide, comfortable grip for your hand. They are a boon for arthritis sufferers and serious shoppers alike.

Send: $2.00 postage & handling

Ask For: Plastic bag carriers

Mail To: Finger Savers
Rt. 1, Box 200
Sinton, TX 78387

Juice-Box Holder

PLASTIC PROTECTION

You want to start packing your kids' lunch sacks with some cardboard containers of fresh fruit juice, but something tells you that those flimsy boxes will get crushed or pop open long before lunchtime arrives. Not to worry. Send for the new **JoosBox,** a plastic holder which prevents squeezing, squirting or spilling. There's also a handy hole on top for a straw.

Send: $1.25 postage & handling

Ask For: JoosBox Holder

Mail To: C&F Distributors
475 North Broome Avenue
Lindenhurst, NY 11757

• • • • • • • • • • • • • • • • •
Postcard Kit
PICTURE-PERFECT HOBBY

Get started in deltiology, or postcard collecting, with this **beginner's postcard kit and sheet of information** on the hobby that will help you learn about history, art, architecture, geography, and other subjects.

You'll receive five postcards from different eras and places, and an information sheet.

Send: $1.50 postage & handling

Ask For: Beginner postcard kit and information on postcard collecting

Mail To: Joan Nykorchuk
13236 North Seventh Street, No. 4
Suite 237
Phoenix, AZ 85022

• • • • • • • • • • • • • • • • •
Pouring Spout
POUR EXCUSE

You'll have no excuse for not drinking juice or milk sold in paper-sealed cartons when you have one of these useful and durable **Spik-It gadgets.**

Dishwasher-safe and made in the U.S.A., the patented, reusable Spik-It is a 2" pour spout that easily twists into cartons and most plastic container tops as well.

Spik-It provides better control over pouring so that you can avoid drips and spills. Its easy-to-remove cap also prevents broken fingernails and further aggravation to arthritic fingers.

Send: $1.50 postage & handling for one; $2.00 for two

Ask For: Spik-It

Mail To: Jaye Products, Inc.
P.O. Box 10726
Naples, FL 33941

● ● ● ● ● ● ● ● ● ● ● ● ● ● ● ● ●

Window Decals

DON'T FORGET

"You Are Not Forgotten." These words, displayed along with the stark silhouetted image of a lone prisoner of war on this **POW/MIA window decal,** serve as a poignant reminder of our American brothers who were POWs or declared missing in action in the Vietnam War.

This 3" x 4" decal honors the brave soldiers. The supplier of these decals, a veteran himself, is not asking for any contributions, just your concern.

Send:	A long SASE
Ask For:	POW/MIA decals
Mail To:	POW/MIA Decals 4230 POW's/MIA's Memorial Drive St. Cloud, FL 34772-8142
Limit:	Three per household

● ● ● ● ● ● ● ● ● ● ● ● ● ● ● ● ●

Magic Trick

PRESTO, CHANGE-GO

Here's a neat trick that involves making money appear and disappear. No, it's not getting a paycheck and paying bills. With this **Chinese magic wallet trick** you can command a coin to vanish, then reappear. The 2" x 3" wallet comes with complete instructions for astounding your friends and family.

Send:	$1.65 postage & handling
Ask For:	Chinese magic wallet trick
Mail To:	Eagle Magic & Joke Store 708 Portland Avenue South Minneapolis, MN 55415

Pumpkin Pie Spice
SPICY DEAL

Variety is the spice of life, and this mixture of various fragrant ingredients will certainly spice up four ordinary pumpkin pies and turn them into blue-ribbon desserts.

Containing secret proportions of cinnamon, ginger, nutmeg, allspice, mace, and cloves, **Mrs. Hamlen's pumpkin pie spice and recipe** have won fame nationwide.

Send: $1.00 postage & handling

Ask For: Mrs. Hamlen's pumpkin pie spice and pie recipe

Mail To: Alaska Craft
P.O. Box 11-1102
Dept. PI/S
Anchorage, AK 99511

Cat Lover's Newsletter
PURR-SUASIVE PROPAGANDA

Attention all fans of felines: this offer for an issue of the brand-new ***Purr-fect Purr-suader®* newsletter** will certainly "cat-alyze" your interest in cat health and nutrition issues.

Devoted to cat topics, the publication includes veterinary advice, fun feline facts, recipes for gourmet cat food, and craft patterns that feature felines. Send for a complimentary issue.

Send: A long SASE

Ask For: Sample issue of *Purr-fect Purr-suader* newsletter

Mail To: Jansen & Co.
P.O. Box 85-CAT
Monterey Park, CA 91754-0085

Sewing Patterns

COUNTRY TOTES

Where would we be without apples and tomatoes? No apple pie, no spaghetti sauce, and no designs for artists and seamstresses. We wouldn't even have these terrific **patterns for an apple tote or a tomato pincushion tote.**

You can send for these complete patterns printed on card stock and featuring full-color photos of the 4" x 5" and 4" x 6" batting-filled fruits. The apple pattern also includes a pattern for a 2" x 3" apple magnet.

Send: $1.95 postage & handling for each pattern

Ask For: Tote pattern
(specify pincushion tote or apple tote)

Mail To: The Pattern Peddler
P.O. Box 1485
Valparaiso, IN 46384

Refunding Newsletter

GET SOME CENTS

Save up to 40 percent on your grocery bills—and receive such free items as film, baby formula, dishes, and more. How?

Read **Refunding Makes Cents,** an 88-page newsletter that lists coupon and refund offers and gives subscribers the opportunity to place ads for trading or buying refund forms and other types of deals. You'll soon learn that refunding can become a profession in itself!

Send: $1.00 postage & handling

Ask For: Sample issue of *Refunding Makes Cents*

Mail To: *Refunding Makes Cents*
P.O. Box R-FB
Farmington, UT 84025

Baby Supplies Catalog & Bottle Sample

FEEDING TIME FOR TODDLERS

Here's an offer that's perfect for new parents. You can order a four-ounce **baby bottle and a catalog.**

These Remond for Babies bottles are hygienic, easy to use, and designed to help prevent aerophagia. Although the bottles cost $2.00 plus postage and handling, you'll get a $2.00 refund when you place your first order. The catalog contains everything from rattles to pacifiers.

Send: $3.50 (includes bottle)

Ask For: Four-ounce sample bottle and catalog

Mail To: Remond for Babies
6105 Portal Way
Ferndale, WA 98248

Reye's Syndrome Brochures

MEDICAL MYSTERY

A person's life can depend on early diagnosis of Reye's Syndrome, a disease with an unknown cause.

As explained in the four-page brochure **Reye's Syndrome: Because You Need to Know,** the illness often follows a virus and most lethally affects the liver and brain. Because aspirin seems to be associated with the syndrome's development, children under age 19 suffering from viruses should avoid medications listed on the flyer titled **Preparations Containing Aspirin.**

Send: Your name & address

Ask For: *Reye's Syndrome: Because You Need to Know* and *Preparations Containing Aspirin*

Mail To: National Reye's Syndrome Foundation
P.O. Box 829 F   Or call toll-free:
Bryan, OH 43506   1-800-233-7393

• • • • • • • • • • • • • • • • •

Laundry Guide

FOR THOSE LAUNDRY-DAY BLUES

You'll soon be singing "Wash away those laundry day blues" when you have a copy of the **Rit Dye and Fabric Treatment Guide to Fabric Care.** In these tough economic times, replacing ruined clothing is the last thing you want to do. This guide gives valuable laundering and stain-removal tips, common laundry dilemmas and their causes, and easy solutions on how to properly maintain clothing and fabric.

Send: Your name & address

Ask For: *The Rit Dye and Fabric Treatment Guide to Fabric Care*

Mail To: RIT Dye, Dept. 230
P.O. Box 307
Coventry, CT 06238

• • • • • • • • • • • • • • • • •

Do-It-Yourself Rose Arbor Plans

A BACKYARD SANCTUARY

All homeowners know the best way to increase the value of their home is with additions and improvements. But a contractor can be expensive.

Whether you plan to sell in the near future or just want to spruce up your surroundings, building an old-fashioned rose arbor in your yard might be a worthwhile project. All you need are basic woodworking skills and these **instructions.**

Send: 50 cents postage & handling

Ask For: Old-fashioned rose arbor plans

Mail To: Western Wood Products Assn., Dept. F
Yeon Building
522 Southwest Fifth Avenue
Portland, OR 97204-2122

Cat Toy & Catalog

PUSSYCAT PLAYTHINGS

If you want to keep your cat off the prowl and in the house, maybe you need to amuse kitty with some new toys. Send in now for a **sample catnip cat toy and a catalog** of other such playthings. You'll find catnip-filled olives and flannel blankets among the many items available through the catalog.

Send: $2.75 postage & handling

Ask For: Cat toy & catalog

Mail To: SATRA'S Purr Palace
Route 1, Box 21
Whitewater, WI 53190

Cookbook

SEA FARE

Everyone tells us that fish is good for us; it's low in calories, low in fat, and low in cholesterol—except when we cook it in oil or butter. So how can we **prepare** fish so that it remains healthful? Check this 224-page **recipe book** titled *Seafood: A Collection of Heart-Healthy Recipes.*

Send: $5.50 for cookbook

Ask For: Seafood cookbook

Mail To: National Seafood Educators
P.O. Box 60006
Richmond Beach, WA 98160

Shopping Guide
SHOP OUT

The Joy of Outlet Shopping, a **200-page book,** will show you where you can find factory outlet centers and stores throughout the country. The directory also includes coupons, shopping tips, and a sales-tax guide.

For a list of one particular state's outlet shopping centers, all you need to do is send a self-addressed stamped envelope with a request for the particular state you would like.

Send:	A long SASE with a request for a particular state, or $4.95 for the book
Ask For:	*The Joy of Outlet Shopping*
Mail To:	*The Joy of Outlet Shopping* P.O. Box 17129, Dept. FB Clearwater, FL 34622-0129

Gourmet Coffee Sample
FLAVORED COFFEE

For a change of pace, coffee drinkers may want to try one of the many **flavored coffees** available in this offer. You can choose from Mocha Java, Kona Blend, Vanilla Nut Cream, or California Orange.

You'll receive a two-ounce sample of the coffee you request and an order form for other special blends. Please indicate if you would like whole beans or ground coffee. The sample is enough to make a full ten-cup pot.

Send:	$1.50 postage & handling
Ask For:	Specify coffee flavor and whole bean or ground
Mail To:	Signature Coffee Company P.O. Box 1789-F Redway, CA 95560

Sample Tea Bags

TEA FOR TWO

For a tasty sample of organic tea, be sure to send in your request for this offer. You'll receive **two sample tea bags** featuring the flavor of your choice and an order form for these and other flavors.

Choose Green Tea, Breakfast Tea, Earl Grey, Toasted Ban-Cha, or Orange Spice Tea.

Send: 50 cents postage & handling

Ask For: Specify tea flavor

Mail To: Signature Coffee Company
P.O. Box 1789-F
Redway, CA 95560

Simmering Potpourri

AUTUMN AROMAS

Fill your home with the fragrance of natural spices, herbs, and fruits. Simply add to one cup of water a tablespoon from this **one-ounce sample of Simmering Scents Potpourri.** Then simmer the mixture on your stove and fill your kitchen with the fragrance of Harvest Apple Pie or Autumn Citrus Spice.

You'll also receive recipes to make your own simmering potpourri plus a price list of natural botanical ingredients.

Send: $1.00 postage & handling

Ask For: One-ounce sample of Simmering Scents Potpourri plus a price list of natural botanical ingredients (choose from Harvest Apple Pie or Autumn Citrus Spice scents)

Mail To: The Gifted Rose
P.O. Box 511
Port Townsend, WA 98368

• • • • • • • • • • • • • • • • • •

Information Kit

VERTICAL AVIATION

Yes, you can jump out of an airplane this weekend. That is, if you send for this information kit about skydiving. Skydiving is not just falling, it is flying. Sport parachuting is no longer a rough-and-tumble sport. New equipment and training techniques let you advance quickly to graceful freefall, swift and controlled canopy flight, and smooth, easy tiptoe landings.

The information you'll receive includes **descriptions of the three courses of skydiving instruction** and lists the 300 parachuting schools across North America.

Send: Your name & address

Ask For: Skydiving information kit

Mail To: Parachute Industry Association
P.O. Box 4232-963
Santa Barbara, CA 93140-4232

• • • • • • • • • • • • • • • • • •

Consumer Guide

NIGHTY NIGHT

Do you wake up feeling weary? Wonder why?

Consult the interesting, thorough consumer guide called *The Sleep Better, Live Better Guide.* The 24-page publication explains the different stages of sleep, describes 10 ways to sleep better, lists tips for buying a good mattress, suggests ways to combat insomnia, and offers information on common sleep disturbances.

Send: Your name & address

Ask For: *The Sleep Better, Live Better Guide*

Mail To: Better Sleep Council
P.O Box 13
Washington, DC 20044

Social Security Card

A LIFETIME SUPPLY

Did you know that your paper social security card is actually the property of the government? This attractive three-color **Social Security Card** is engraved with your name and social security number and is guaranteed to last a lifetime—it will not burn, break, or fade. It's the size of a credit card and will easily fit into your wallet or purse. A practical gift idea for you or for friends.

Send: $2.00 postage & handling

Ask For: Social Security Card (carefully print the name— using no more than 25 letters & spaces—and Social Security number you want engraved.)

Mail To: Great Tracers
3 Schoenbeck Road
Prospect Heights, IL 60070-1435

Detergent Sample

SOAP TO GO

Toss this **portion pack of SOPAX laundry detergent** in your washer and watch your clothes get whiter, brighter, and softer. The biodegradable, phosphate-free detergent, which comes in a water-soluble packet, is an incredibly convenient, effective way to do laundry.

A flyer accompanying your sample will tell you how to obtain more packets of the economical powder.

Send: A long SASE

Ask For: Portion pack of SOPAX detergent

Mail To: Frank Hinton, Jr.
1622 Hunter's Trail
Rock Hill, SC 29732

• • • • • • • • • • • • • • • • •

Catalog of Special Clothes for Special Children

KID'S CLOTHING

It has always been hard to find clothes for children with special needs. Finally, there is an easy way to shop for these special kids.

The items included in this **catalog** are made of only the highest-quality materials and designed to be both stylish and functional. There are clothing items with Velcro closures, snap crotches, and snap-on bibs. Many garments are available in a variety of colors.

Send: $1.00 postage & handling

Ask For: Catalog of special clothes for special children

Mail To: Special Clothes
P.O. Box 4220
Alexandria, VA 22303

• • • • • • • • • • • • • • • • •

Special Day Art Stamp & Catalog

A BIRTHDAY BASH

Every time you throw a birthday party for your children, you seem to have a hard time finding the right invitations. Now you can create your own with an **art design rubber stamp** that reads "Special Day." Order this $4.50 value and receive a catalog for other rubber stamps and supplies currently available.

Send: $2.00 postage & handling

Ask For: "Special Day" art stamp & catalog

Mail To: The Stamp Pad Company, Inc.
P.O. Box 43
Dept. FK
Big Lake, MN 55309

Spice Rack Plans & Catalog

SPICE UP YOUR KITCHEN

You probably haven't used a washboard in years, but with these **instructions** you'll learn how to turn one into a practical spice rack for your kitchen. Your finished spice rack washboard can also be used as a note board with magnets and a place to hang your keys. You'll also receive a catalog of other do-it-yourself kits and supplies.

Send: $1.00 postage & handling

Ask For: Free spice rack washboard plans & catalog

Mail To: Cherry Tree Toys, Inc.
Spice Rack Washboard Plan
P.O. Box 369-135SR
Belmont, OH 43718

Organizer

BAG FOR BAGS

Here's a clever, decorative way to keep plastic grocery bags ready for reuse. Called **The Stasher,** this fabric drawstring bag allows you to insert bags from the top and dispense them individually from the elasticized opening at the bottom.

Handcrafted from attractive decorator fabric and measuring 13" long, the bag holds up to 20 plastic grocery bags and can hang by its ribbon drawstring from a doorknob or a hook.

Send: $2.00 postage & handling for each

Ask For: The Stasher

Mail To: Southwest Savvy
P.O. Box 1361-FB
Apple Valley, CA 92307

●●●●●●●●●●●●●●●●●●●

Comic-Style Booklet

CHECK IT OUT

Do you ever wonder how the slender pieces of paper we call checks help you pay your bills and then end up in the account statement from your bank? Do you know who invented paper checks? Find out by reading the comic-style booklet called *The Story of Checks and Electronic Payments.*

Published by the Federal Reserve Bank of New York, the 24-page educational booklet presents interesting information about our country's banking system.

Send: Your name & address

Ask For: *The Story of Checks*

Mail To: Federal Reserve Bank of New York
33 Liberty Street
New York, NY 10045

●●●●●●●●●●●●●●●●●●

Dart Shaftite

ON TARGET

This new product is right on target for dart aficionados. Get a complimentary sample of **Shaftite.** A $3.00 value, this amazing accessory eliminates forever the annoying distraction of loose dart shafts.

This rubber gripper securely holds any 2BA dart shaft for years. The supplier, Strad Darts, will also reveal other creative ideas to help you improve your darting techniques and enjoyment.

Send: A long SASE

Ask For: Dart Shaftite

Mail To: Strad Darts, Dept. M
P.O. Box 602
Westboro, MA 01581

Limit: One per long SASE

Denture Adhesive

STUCK ON YOU

Send for this free sample of KLUTCH **denture adhesive powder** and see how well it holds your dentures in place. Made from two natural gums, the adhesive has superlong holding power that reportedly outlasts its competitors. The generous .75-oz. sample is attractively packaged in a quaint blue tin.

Send: $2.00 postage & handling

Ask For: Free sample of KLUTCH denture adhesive powder

Mail To: I. Putnam, Inc.
Dept. FBS
P.O. Box 444
Big Flats, NY 14814

Guide for Teens

HELP FOR STUTTERERS

Do you stutter?

That question is part of the title of this reassuring, informative publication that addresses teenagers who stutter. Written by eight speech experts, the 80-page *Do You Stutter: A Guide for Teens* provides plenty of solid counsel for kids who suffer from stuttering and who may cope with negative behavior from parents, teachers and friends. The guide also helps teenagers decide whether they need therapy—and it includes cartoons from Greg Evans's comic strip *Luann*.

Send: $1.00 postage & handling

Ask For: *Do You Stutter: A Guide for Teens*

Mail To: Stuttering Foundation of America
P.O. Box 11749
Memphis, TN 38111-0749

• • • • • • • • • • • • • • • • •

Miniature Quilt Pattern

SUMMER SNUGGLE

This lovely miniature quilt will bring a bit of the warmth of summer into your home. Easy-to-follow **instructions and pattern** templates make up this pattern for a summer basket quilt.

The finished quilt measures 15" x 22" and features a geometric design of six gift baskets. It makes a beautiful wall hanging for your favorite room or a great gift for your best friend. It's also a nice accessory for doll collectors.

Send:	$1.00 postage & handling
Ask For:	Kay's summer basket quilt pattern
Mail To:	Elaine's
	P.O. Box 751558
	Dept. FB KSB
	Petaluma, CA 94975-1558

• • • • • • • • • • • • • • • • •

Sweet Potato Recipe Booklet

TASTY TREATS

If a sweet potato–sausage casserole or sweet potato stuffing sounds like the perfect addition to your next dinner menu, then you'll want to peruse this booklet filled with these and other **tasty recipes.** The booklet covers dozens of sweet potato recipes for salads, desserts, and main dishes.

Send:	A long SASE with 52 cents postage affixed
Ask For:	Sweet potato recipe booklet
Mail To:	Harold H. Hoecker
	SPC-F92
	P.O. Box 14
	McHenry, MD 21541-0014

Patterns for T-Shirt Tie

HOT TEE

Get in on a hot fashion trend with these **T-shirt tie patterns** in sizzling Southwest designs. Even if you don't have the means to craft this T-shirt tie out of wood as directed, you can still use the patterns to create fabulous fabric appliqués.

Each pattern includes detailed directions. The five patterns that you will receive are for Howlin' Coyote, Saguaro Cactus, Chili Pepper, Cowboy Boot, and Potted Prickly Pear Cactus ties.

Send: $2.00 postage & handling for five

Ask For: T-shirt tie patterns

Mail To: Southwest Savvy
P.O. Box 1361 FB
Apple Valley, CA 92307

Lake Tahoe Cross-Country Ski-Trail Map

TAHOE NORDIC SKI TRAILS

Not everyone travels to Lake Tahoe in the winter for the area's famous downhill ski runs. More people are discovering the allure of Nordic skiing, and Lake Tahoe offers some scenic trails for cross-country enthusiasts. This colorful **brochure and trail map** cover all the Nordic ski excursions available at this popular winter vacation destination.

Send: Your name & address

Ask For: Tahoe Nordic brochure

Mail To: Tahoe Nordic
P.O. Box 1632
Tahoe City, CA 96145

● ● ● ● ● ● ● ● ● ● ● ● ● ● ● ● ●

Hiking Brochure

TAKE A HIKE

We mean that in the nicest way possible. In fact, before you hit the hiking trails, we suggest you read this **eight-panel brochure** titled *Hiking Safety.*

It provides general safety guidelines as well as specialized information on such topics as crossing rivers, avoiding hypothermia, and dealing with bears, snakes and poisonous insects. So take care, and happy trails to you.

Send: Your name & address

Ask For: Hiking Safety brochure

Mail To: American Hiking Society
P.O. Box 20160
Washington, DC 20041-2160

● ● ● ● ● ● ● ● ● ● ● ● ● ● ● ● ●

Catalog

HOME IMPROVEMENTS

Anyone who has a hobby involving woodworking, homebuilding, needle arts, or gardening will love this **catalog.** It is brimming with exciting new titles and established best sellers. All titles are the work of experts in the field who share their best ideas and discoveries with fellow enthusiasts. It is published by the same folks who publish *Fine Woodworking, Fine Homebuilding, Threads,* and *Fine Gardening* magazines.

Send: Your name & address

Ask For: Book and video catalog

Mail To: The Taunton Press
63 South Main Street
P.O. Box 5506
Newtown, CT 06470-5506

Discount Pharmaceuticals

INEXPENSIVE, NOT CHEAP

Low prices, high quality, and customer satisfaction are guaranteed with every prescription and vitamin order from the **TBN Pharmaceutical mail-order program.** TBN customers are guaranteed to receive the lowest prices. Should you find a lower price, the TBN program will match that price. Prepayment is not required; you can be invoiced or pay by credit card. If you are not satisfied with your order for any reason, you can return unopened items for a 100 percent refund, replacement, or credit. Order this catalog and receive a $5.00 discount coupon on your first order.

Send: $1.95 postage & handling

Ask For: TBN Pharmaceutical catalog & coupon

Mail To: The Buying Network (TBN)
P.O. Box 85619
Richmond, VA 23285-5619

Texas Peanut Producers Kids Club

MAKE YOUR KIDS NUTS

Maybe there are times when your children make you nuts. Here's your chance to turn the tables on them. Sign the kids up as members of the Texas Peanut Producers **Kids Club.** They'll receive a membership certificate, collectible stickers, and a recipe brochure. Peanuts make a healthy snack, and your children will get several ideas on how to serve them up.

Send: $1.00 postage & handling

Ask For: Texas Peanut Producers Kids Club

Mail To: Texas Peanuts
1008 Second Street
Old Sacramento, CA 95814

Tollhouse Cookies

A SWEET OFFER

Satisfy that sweet tooth with America's favorite taste treat. Tollhouse **cookies** have been a popular snack since they were first served by Ruth Graves Wakefield more than 50 years ago at the Toll House Restaurant in Massachusetts. Send in and you'll receive a two-ounce sample of a special Tollhouse variety in your choice of flavors. You may choose between the Gourmet Chocolate Chip or the Peanut Butter–Chocolate Chip Cookie.

Send: $2.00 postage & handling

Ask For: Specify Gourmet Chocolate Chip or Peanut Butter–Chocolate Chip cookies

Mail To: Toll House Bakery Gourmet Cookie Offer
P.O. Box 457
Whitman, MA 02382

Tomato Tree Seeds

UP A TREE

Tomatoes on a tree? Sound unbelievable? Not if you've been to South America and seen this native tree, up to ten feet tall, that is grown for its fruit. But you don't have to head south for the winter. This supplier will send you your very own **packet of tomato tree seeds.**

The tomato tree can be grown indoors or out, potted or in the ground. It makes a fun houseplant that produces large, exotic leaves, fragrant flowers, then beautiful red fruit for up to five months a year.

Send: $1.00 postage & handling

Ask For: Tomato tree seeds

Mail To: Tomato Tree
P.O. Box 3498
San Rafael, CA 94902

• • • • • • • • • • • • • • • • • •

Trip Planner

TRAVELIN' TWOSOME

To help travel companions who want to organize their vacation time and money before they depart, American Express has published the helpful, foldout travel planner called *Vacations Built for Two.*

The planner offers three sections: tips for planning a trip, an organizer in which to note detailed travel arrangements, and "Hot Spots for Travel Companions," a Gallup Poll list of destinations favored by traveling twosomes.

Send: Your name & address

Ask For: *Vacations Built for Two*

Mail To: *Vacations Built for Two* Travel Planner
P.O. Box 2300
New Brunswick, NJ 08903

• • • • • • • • • • • • • • • • • •

Fruit & Vegetable
Poster

GOING TROPICAL

You want to spice up your next meal with something a little different than peas and carrots or apples and oranges. Then why not pick up some tropical fruits and vegetables included on this **foldout poster.**

With a full-color photo and information on each item, the foldout poster serves as a guide to the availability and nutritional value of various out-of-the-ordinary fruits and vegetables.

Send: Your name & address

Ask For: Tropical fruit & vegetable poster

Mail To: Stephanie Johnson
J.R. Brooks & Son
P.O. Drawer 9
Homestead, FL 33090

• • • • • • • • • • • • • • • • •

Catalog & Newsletter

TAKE A PEEK

If cherry pie reminds you of Agent Dale Cooper, and if dictaphones make you want to speak to someone named Diane, you're a genuine *Twin Peaks* freak who absolutely needs a copy of **Twin Peaks Speaks catalog & newsletter.**

Fans of the two-season television show and the film will discover in the catalog all kinds of paraphernalia related to the bizarre media phenomenon created by director David Lynch.

Send: $1.00 postage & handling

Ask For: *Twin Peaks Speaks* catalog & newsletter

Mail To: Twin Peaks Press
P.O. Box 129
Vancouver, WA 98666-0129

• • • • • • • • • • • • • • • • •

Pet Catalog

ANIMAL ESSENTIALS

If you'd like to find a complete pet store just sitting in your mailbox, then you'll want to request **UPCO's 160-page catalog of pet items** at wholesale prices.

In business for 40 years, UPCO (United Pharmacal Company) carries more than 5,000 products for dogs, cats, birds, horses, and pet rodents.

Send: Your name & address

Ask For: UPCO catalog of pet items

Mail To: UPCO
Dept. F
P.O. Box 969
St. Joseph, MO 64502

Government Book Catalog
AMERICA'S BOOKSTORE

The largest publisher in the United States is...the United States. The Government Printing Office produces numerous books and pamphlets for all government agencies, and the majority of them are available to the public.

This **catalog of government books** lists publications in such subject areas as business and industry, history, hobbies, and space exploration. Sample titles include *Travel Tips for Older Americans* and *Starting and Managing a Business From Your Home.*

Send: Your name & address

Ask For: U.S. government books catalog

Mail To: New Catalog–FB
P.O. Box 37000
Washington, DC 20401

Cents-Off Couponing Guide
SUPER-MARKET SAVINGS

With the high price of grocery shopping, taking a few moments to clip out coupons from magazine ads or newspaper inserts can add up to big savings. In fact, many markets now offer double coupon credits. Send for this *Guide to Cents-Off Couponing* and learn the facts, figures, and shopping strategies that make couponing a popular pursuit for many savvy shoppers.

Send: A long SASE

Ask For: Guide to Cents-Off Couponing

Mail To: Valassis Inserts
c/o Public Relations Free Offer
36111 Schoolcraft Road
Livonia, MI 48154

Energy Booklet

DRIVING FOR DOLLARS

Did you know that octane is not a measure of a fuel's power? Or that an underinflated tire can increase fuel consumption?

Learn many more facts about how you can run your car responsibly; request the government's interesting 14-page booklet called *Energy Conservation Information for Vehicle Owners.*

Send: Your name & address

Ask For: *Energy Conservation Information for Vehicle Owners*

Mail To: CAREIRS   Or call toll-free:
P.O. Box 8900   1-800-523-2929
Silver Spring, MD 20907

Maple Sprinkles

MAPLE TREAT

Vermont country would like to treat you to **two sample packets of Maple Sprinkles.** Maple Sprinkles—100% pure maple sugar—the best all-natural sweetener in the world!

Produced by a patented process that combines tradition and technology, Maple Sprinkles gives you pure organic maple syrup in a dry granulated form.

Sweeten all your recipes, and create exciting healthful dishes and baked goods without white sugar. A catalog shows you how to order more Maple Sprinkles.

Send: A long SASE

Ask For: Two packets of Maple Sprinkles

Mail To: Vermont Country Maple, Inc.
P.O. Box 53-F
Jericho Center, VT 05465

•••••••••••••••••••

British Vouchers

A CAPITAL IDEA

Currency collectors should jump at the chance to obtain this valuable **set of four British armed forces special vouchers** that have never been circulated. Collectors have been paying much more for the £1 note (Second Series, 1950) and the 5, 10, and 50 new pence notes (Sixth Series, 1972).

Used by British military personnel to purchase items at canteens or post exchanges, the vouchers make a capital investment for American collectors.

Send: $2.00 postage & handling

Ask For: Four British armed forces special vouchers

Mail To: JOLIE
P.O. Box 144
Roslyn Heights, NY 11577-0144

•••••••••••••••••••

Recipe Brochure

APPLE INSPIRATIONS

No wonder an apple provoked the fall of Eve and Adam; its crunchy texture and lovely colors invite sampling.

Apples also entice gourmet cooks to combine the fruit with other fresh foods; and the great chefs featured in the beautifully prepared **Romance of Flavors recipe brochure** have done just that. Eight top chefs from around the country share their apple-oriented inspirations in this 12-page, full-color publication.

Send: A long SASE with 52 cents postage affixed

Ask For: *The Romance of Flavors*

Mail To: Washington Apple Commission
P.O. Box 550ROF-FB
Wenatchee, WA 98807

• • • • • • • • • • • • • • • •

Plastic Guards
WATCH OUT

If you use your hands a lot, or if you're simply prone to mishaps, you'll want to request this useful **watch guard assortment.**

Developed for a famous Swiss watchmaker, the plastic guards, which fit watches of all sizes, protect watch crystals against scratches and breakage.

Your assortment will include five different colors to complement your timepiece and brighten your wardrobe.

Send: $2.00 postage & handling

Ask For: Watch guard assortment

Mail To: Gary Martel
5436 Granada Way
Carpinteria, CA 93013

• • • • • • • • • • • • • • • •

Personalized Cards
WHAT'S THIS FUNNY BUSINESS?

This service is All In Fun and it's perfect for the person who has everything (including a sense of humor). In the weeks leading up to their birthday, All In Fun will send any person you designate a series of humorous, personalized postcards. Each card will carry a funny message and illustration along with a unique postmark. Write for a **sample humorous birthday postcard and information.**

Send: A long SASE

Ask For: Sample humorous birthday postcard & information

Mail To: All In Fun
P.O. Box 152
Collinsville, IL 62234

White House Tour Book

PRESIDENTIAL ADDRESS

You don't have to wait for the next State of the Union address to hear from our leader. Just drop a line to 1600 Pennsylvania Avenue and ask for **The White House Tour Book.**

This 32-page, glossy, full-color book takes you on a tour through every room of the White House with fascinating information and beautiful photographs.

It also includes notes about our government and interesting and educational articles.

Send: Your name & address

Ask For: Photo tour booklet

Mail To: The White House
Washington, DC 20500

Holiday Recipes

TRIMMED TREATS

If you like to celebrate fall and winter holidays by helping your family make scrumptious desserts and party foods, you'll love these **Halloween and/or Christmas idea folders.**

Each ten-panel folder carries full-color photos of delectably decorated foods plus recipes and ideas to make your autumn memorable. Request one or both from Wilton Enterprises, experts in the field of dessert decorating.

Send: A long SASE

Ask For: Halloween and/or Christmas ideas and recipes

Mail To: Wilton Enterprises Consumer Affairs
2240 West 75th Street
Woodridge, IL 60517

Christmas Ornament

WOODEN WHIMSY

Handmade decorations, like this **mitten or stocking wooden ornament,** add a warm touch to a Christmas tree. They contribute a bit of nostalgia to festivities, and they invite us to take time to celebrate the moment.

Painted in red and green with accent colors, each of the ornaments offered here measures about 2" long.

Send: $2.00 postage & handling

Ask For: Wooden ornament (specify stocking or mitten)

Mail To: Mommy & Me Crafts
P.O. Box 755
Burleson, TX 76028

Clothing Care Guide

WOOL'S WORTH

During tough economic times, many of us choose to purchase quality items that will last for a while, such as wool clothing and upholstery. Our knowing how to care for this natural fiber helps to protect our fabric assets.

That's why you'll appreciate this **two-sided wallet card** titled "Your Guide for Wool Clothing Care." One side of the plastic card will assist you with spot and stain removal, and the other side lists tips for maintaining wool garments.

Send: A long SASE

Ask For: Wool care card

Mail To: The Wool Bureau, Inc.
360 Lexington Avenue, Seventh Floor
New York, NY 10017

Limit: One per address

200 Postage Stamps

Fun Philately

Stamp out ignorance of world geography; start a stimulating stamp collection with this **super worldwide collection of 200 postage stamps.**

You'll receive a splendid assortment of international stamps that will spark your interest in philately, or stamp collecting, as well as in art, history, sports, entertainment, and lots of other subjects.

Send: $2.00 postage & handling

Ask For: Super worldwide collection of 200 stamps

Mail To: Universal
P.O. Box 466
Port Washington, NY 11050

Phone Message

Wrong Number

With all the things going wrong in the world, you almost need a scorecard to keep track of the mess. That's the idea that led Janet Pensig to start her **Glitch Phone Report.**

Every week Pensig records a new two-minute phone message about what is going wrong with technology, the environment, and other areas of life. Glitch has been featured on the nationally syndicated radio show *The Osgood File* and in the *New York Post*. The call is free except for normal long-distance charges if calling from outside of New York City.

Phone: (212) 228-7514

Listen To: Glitch Phone Report

••••••••••••••••••

Pamphlet &
newsletter

FRAME THE FUN

Bowling is a ball, according to Bif, a character who demonstrates proper bowling techniques in **Bif's Fundamentals of Bowling,** a pamphlet aimed at ages 3 to 21. Bif also invites you to join the Young American Bowling Alliance, which sponsors leagues and competitions.

The eight-page newsletter called *Framework* contains helpful hints and news about other youth bowlers.

Send: A long SASE for *Bif's Fundamentals of Bowling* and a postcard for *Framework*

Ask For: *Bif's Fundamentals of Bowling* and/or *Framework*

Mail To: Young American Bowling Alliance
Attention Bif and Buzzy
5301 South 76th Street
Greendale, WI 53129

••••••••••••••••••

Pattern

DEER SANTA...

Let Santa know that you're awaiting his arrival; post a lighted Christmas deer ornament in your front yard.

This full-size **pattern for a wooden deer yard ornament** comes with instructions and a photo so that you can cut and put together the 12" head that resembles Rudolph with his red nose. Place him on the 15" stick so that Santa and his elves are sure to spot your house.

Send: $1.95 postage & handling

Ask For: Christmas pattern for a wooden deer yard ornament

Mail To: Unique Patterns
Route 1, Box 154
Department F
Waynesville, MO 65583

Zipper Lubricant

ZIPPING ALONG

It's the big night of the party, and though you're ready for the occasion, the zipper on your favorite dress won't budge. Don't risk breaking it by trying to force it. All you need is a of couple of drops of **Zipper-go®** to make that zipper slide.

This amazing lubricant works instantly to undo stuck zippers. Use on dresses, jackets, backpacks, and more. The half-oz. sample will keep you zipping along for a long time.

Send: $2.00 postage & handling

Ask For: Zipper-Go®

Mail To: Zipper-Go®
P.O. Box 3481
Escondido, CA 92033

Gift Basket
Instructions

GIVE SOMETHING SPECIAL

When the Christmas holiday is approaching, and once again you're stumped over what special gift to give your special friends. Show you care by putting together a **homemade gift basket.**

Making a gift basket is easier than you think when you send off for these instructions and illustrations. You can pick up all the products you'll need to complete your basket at a craft or grocery store.

Send: A long SASE with 52 cents postage affixed

Ask For: Gift basket instructions

Mail To: Carol Starr
8045 Antoine
P.O. Box 147
Houston, TX 77088

• • • • • • • • • • • • • • • • • •

Vacation Information

PLACES TO GO, PEOPLE TO SEE

Approximately 120 miles from Washington, D.C. sits the unique Shenandoah Valley. Located here are ski areas, day trips to historical sites, Shenandoah National Park, George Washington National Forest, Endless Caverns, and many antiques stores. These are just some of the features described in the free **information packet** from the Harrisonburg and Rockingham County Chamber of Commerce. The past and present all come together in this unique vacation spot.

Send: A long SASE

Ask For: Harrisonburg and Rockingham visitor information in the heart of the Shenandoah Valley

Mail To: Harrisonburg and Rockingham County Chamber of Commerce P.O. Box 1 Harrisonburg, VA 22801

• • • • • • • • • • • • • • • • • •

Wooden Figures

BARNYARD KNICK-KNACKS

Display shelves aren't just for books and record albums. A lot of people like to put up decorative **knick-knacks.** Here's a pair of such trinkets that are hand-made and painted. One features a cow in a tub and reads "Milk Bath." The other shows a pig and reads "Hog Wash." Both wooden figures are about 3" in length and 2" high.

Send: $1.75 each

Ask For: Hog Wash and/or Milk Bath figure

Mail To: Mommy & Me Crafts P.O. Box 755 Burleson, TX 76028

Stuffed Animal

DON'T SQUEEZE THE HUGGABLES

They're cute. Adorable. Squeezable. Washable. Huggable.

These 5" stuffed **Huggables** for baby are all this and more. Bunnies, hippos and kitties, elephants and bears. They're pink, mint, peach, and white. Made of resilient polyester with a smooth parachute-like texture, they make a great first friend for a baby. Their features are stitched like old-fashioned cloth dolls.

Dressed in colorful overalls, soft and small, these pals are great for young grips. There are an assortment of huggable animals so you'll receive the supplier's choice.

Send: $2.00 postage & handling

Ask For: Baby animal Huggables

Mail To: Christian Treasures
Huggables
P.O. Box 15
Huntington Beach, CA 92648

Miniature Birdhouses

NOT JUST FOR THE BIRDS

Here's a little something to place on your cabinet or shelves. You can order a set of two **miniature birdhouses,** both made of wood and hand-painted. One stands about 1 -1/2" high and has a single perch, while the second is twice the size and has two perches.

Send: $2.00 postage & handling

Ask For: Set of two birdhouses

Mail To: Mommy & Me Crafts
P.O. Box 755
Burleson, TX 76028

• • • • • • • • • • • • • • • • • •
Pewter Thimbles
NOT FOR SEWING

One of seven animals sits on top of these **pewter animal thimbles.** Watch out—is that a dancing bear or a prancing horse or is it a kitten, a goose, a pig, a cow, or the carousel horse? Each is distinctive and detailed. Normally sold in retail stores for $6.00 each, the supplier will send you one for just $2.00. Add them to your thimble or miniature collections or just display them on a shelf. The supplier will make every attempt to send you the animal of your choice, but at this special price it is their choice.

Send: $2.00 postage & handling

Ask For: Pewter thimble

Mail To: Jewelry by Marsha
Box 2428
Melbourne, FL 32902

• • • • • • • • • • • • • • • • •
Soap Sample
FAVORITE SOAP

Our favorite soap is not *Days of Our Lives*. It's Sierra Soap! This **wonderful soap** is handmade with all natural ingredients like olive and soybean oils, and is gentle enough for people with sensitive skin or allergies.

Sierra Soap is available unscented or in a variety of fragrances. You'll receive a single one-ounce sample bar along with a folksy newsletter.

Send: $1.50 postage & handling

Ask For: Sierra Soap sample

Mail To: Parodon
P.O. Box 1863-F
Pollock Pines, CA 95726

Skin-Care Brochure

SUN DAY SCHOOL

Skin cancer is the most common of all cancers, affects one in every six Americans, and is diagnosed in more than 600,000 Americans every year. The brochure *For Every Child Under the Sun* explains common misconceptions about the sun and skin cancers, how to choose a sunscreen, and ten simple steps that you can take to protect yourself and your family. You are never too young to start taking care of your skin. Remember, almost all skin cancer is preventable.

Send: A long SASE

Ask For: *For Every Child Under the Sun*

Mail To: Skin Cancer Foundation
Box 561
Dept. PAR/F
New York NY 10158

"First Haircut" and "Tooth Fairy" Chests

CLASSY KEEPSAKES

Sometimes you want a little bit more to remember your child's early years than some faded photographs. When your baby gets that first haircut or loses that first tooth, you may want to save those mementos. Instead of sticking them in an envelope or a plastic bag, try these **hand-made cases.** Each case is a little bit bigger than a 50-cent piece in circumference, and both are hand-painted with designs and descriptions.

Send: $1.75 for each

Ask For: First Haircut and/or Tooth Fairy chest

Mail To: Mommy & Me Crafts
P.O. Box 755
Burleson, TX 76028

FAN-TASTIC FREEBIES

Most professional sports franchises have materials that they distribute free to fans. Season schedules and ticket information are usually available. Some teams even give away fan packages that may contain stickers, photos, fan club info, catalogs, and more.

All you need to do is write your favorite team and ask for a fan package. Although not all teams require it, we recommend that you send a long self-addressed stamped envelope to assist with the processing of your request.

Here's another tip. If you want to contact a specific player on your favorite team, address the envelope to his attention. Keep in mind that because of the high volume of fan mail each team receives, it may take six to eight weeks or more for a response. So be a good sport.

We've compiled the addresses of all baseball, basketball, football, and hockey teams. So go and get 'em. But just remember, as in sports contests, you may not always get what you wanted, but you should still have fun!

AMERICAN LEAGUE BASEBALL TEAMS ....

Baltimore Orioles
Memorial Stadium
Baltimore, MD 21218

Boston Red Sox
4 Yawkey Way
Boston, MA 02115

California Angels
P.O. Box 2000
Anaheim, CA 92803

Chicago White Sox
333 W. 35th St.
Chicago, IL 60616

Cleveland Indians
Cleveland Stadium
Cleveland, OH 44114

Detroit Tigers
Public Relations
2121 Trumbull Ave.
Detroit, MI 48216

Kansas City Royals
P.O. Box 419969
Kansas City, MO 64141

Milwaukee Brewers
201 S. 46th St.
Milwaukee, WI 53214

Minnesota Twins
501 Chicago Ave. South
Minneapolis, MN 55415

New York Yankees
Yankee Stadium
Bronx, NY 10451

Oakland Athletics
Oakland Coliseum
Oakland, CA 94621

Seattle Mariners
P.O. Box 4100
Seattle, WA 98104

Texas Rangers
P.O. Box 90111
Arlington, TX 76010

Toronto Blue Jays
Sky Dome, Suite 3200
300 Bremmer Blvd.
Toronto, Ontario
Canada M5V 3B3

NATIONAL LEAGUE BASEBALL TEAMS ....

Atlanta Braves
P.O. Box 4064
Atlanta, GA 30302

Chicago Cubs
Wrigley Field
1060 West Addison St.
Chicago, IL 60613

Cincinnati Reds
100 Riverfront Stadium
Cincinnati, OH 45202

Colorado Rockies
Suite 2100
1700 Broadway
Denver, CO 80290

Florida Marlins
100 NE 3rd Ave
Ft. Lauderdale, FL 33301

Houston Astros
P.O. Box 288
Houston, TX 77001-0288

Los Angeles Dodgers
1000 Elysian Park Ave.
Los Angeles, CA 90012

Montreal Expos
P.O. Box 500, Station M
Montreal, Quebec
Canada H1V 3P2

New York Mets
Shea Stadium
Flushing, NY 11368

Philadelphia Phillies
Veteran Stadium
P.O. Box 7575
Philadelphia, PA 19101

Pittsburgh Pirates
Public Relations
P.O. Box 7000
Pittsburgh, PA 15212

St. Louis Cardinals
250 Stadium Plaza
St. Louis, MO 63102

San Diego Padres
P.O. Box 2000
San Diego, CA 92102

San Francisco Giants
Candlestick Park
San Francisco, CA 94124

NATIONAL BASKETBALL ASSOCIATION ....

Atlanta Hawks
One CNN Center
South Tower, Suite 405
Atlanta, GA 30303

Boston Celtics
151 Merrimac St., 5th Floor
Boston, MA 02114

Charlotte Hornets
Fan Mail, Hive Drive
Charlotte, NC 28217

Chicago Bulls
980 N. Michigan Ave.,
Suite 1600
Chicago, IL 60611-4501

Cleveland Cavaliers
2923 Streetsboro Rd.
Community Relations
Richfield, OH 44286

Dallas Mavericks
Reunion Arena
777 Sports St.
Dallas, TX 75207

Denver Nuggets
1635 Clay St.
Denver, CO 80204

Detroit Pistons
2 Championship Dr.
Auburn Hills, MI 48326

Golden State Warriors
Oakland Coliseum Arena
Oakland, CA 94621-1995

Houston Rockets
P.O. Box 272349
Houston, TX 77277

Indiana Pacers
300 E. Market St.
Indianapolis, IN 46204

Los Angeles Clippers
L.A. Memorial Sports Arena
3939 S. Figueroa
Los Angeles, CA 90037

Los Angeles Lakers
Great Western Forum
P.O. Box 10
Inglewood, CA 90306

Miami Heat
Miami Arena
Miami, FL 33136-4102

Milwaukee Bucks
1001 N. Fourth St.
Milwaukee, WI 53203

Minnesota Timberwolves
600 First Ave. North
Minneapolis, MN 55403

New Jersey Nets
Brendan Byrne Arena
East Rutherford, NJ 07073

New York Knicks
Madison Square Garden
Four Penn Plaza
New York, NY 10001

Orlando Magic
1 Magic Place
Orlando Arena
Orlando, FL 32801

Philadelphia 76ers
Veteran Stadium
P.O. Box 25040
Philadelphia, PA 19147

Phoenix Suns
P.O. Box 1369
Phoenix, AZ 85001

Portland Trail Blazers
700 NE Multnomah St.
Suite 950, Lloyd Bldg.
Portland, OR 97232

Sacramento Kings
1 Sports Parkway
Sacramento, CA 95834

San Antonio Spurs
600 East Market St.
Suite 102
San Antonio, TX 78205

Seattle Supersonics
C-Box 900911
Seattle, WA 98109

Utah Jazz
301 W. South Temple
Salt Lake City, UT 84101

Washington Bullets
Capital Centre
Landover, MD 20785

AMERICAN CONFERENCE FOOTBALL TEAMS ....

Buffalo Bills
One Bills Drive
Orchard Park, NY 14127

Cincinnati Bengals
200 Riverfront Stadium
Cincinnati, OH 45202

Cleveland Browns
Cleveland Stadium
Cleveland, OH 44114

Denver Broncos
13655 E. Dove Valley Pkwy.
Englewood, CO 80112

Houston Oilers
6910 Fannin Street
Houston, TX 77030

Indianapolis Colts
7001 West 56th Street
Indianapolis, IN 46224

Kansas City Chiefs
One Arrowhead Drive
Kansas City, MO 64129

Los Angeles Raiders
332 Center Street
El Segundo, CA 90245

Miami Dolphins
Joe Robbie Stadium
2269 Northwest 199th St.
Miami, FL 33056

New England Patriots
Foxboro Stadium, Route 1
Foxboro, MA 02035

New York Jets
100 Fulton Ave.
Hempstead, NY 11550

Pittsburgh Steelers
Three Rivers Stadium
300 Stadium Circle
Pittsburgh, PA 15212

San Diego Chargers
Jack Murphy Stadium
9449 Friars Road
San Diego, CA 92108

Seattle Seahawks
11220 Northeast 53rd St.
Kirkland, WA 98033

NATIONAL CONFERENCE FOOTBALL TEAMS ·······································

Atlanta Falcons
Suwanee Road at I-85
Suwanee, GA 30174

Chicago Bears
Halas Hall
250 North Washington Rd.
Lake Forest, IL 60045

Dallas Cowboys
Cowboys Center
1 Cowboys Parkway
Irving, TX 75063-4727

Detroit Lions
1200 Featherstone Road
Pontiac, MI 48057

Green Bay Packers
1265 Lombardi Ave.
Green Bay, WI 54304

Los Angeles Rams
2327 West Lincoln Ave.
Anaheim, CA 92801

Minnesota Vikings
9520 Viking Drive
Eden Prairie, MN 55344

New Orleans Saints
1500 Poydras Street
New Orleans, LA 70003

New York Giants
Giants Stadium
East Rutherford, NJ 07073

Philadelphia Eagles
Broad St. & Pattison Ave.
Philadelphia, PA 19148

Phoenix Cardinals
P.O. Box 888
Phoenix, AZ 85001-0888

San Francisco 49ers
4949 Centennial Blvd.
Santa Clara, CA 95054-1229

Tampa Bay Buccaneers
One Buccaneer Place
Tampa, FL 33607

Washington Redskins
P.O. Box 17247
Dulles International Airport
Washington, DC 20041

NATIONAL HOCKEY LEAGUE ....

Boston Bruins
Boston Garden
150 Causeway St.
Boston, MA 02114

Buffalo Sabres
Memorial Auditorium
140 Main St.
Buffalo, NY 14202

Calgary Flames
P.O. Box 1540
Station M
Calgary, Alberta
Canada T2P 3B9

Chicago Black Hawks
Chicago Stadium
1800 W. Madison
Chicago, IL 60612

Detroit Red Wings
600 Civic Center Dr.
Detroit, MI 48226

Edmonton Oilers
Northlands Coliseum
7424-118 Ave.
Edmonton, Alberta,
Canada T5B 4M9

Hartford Whalers
242 Trumbull St
Hartford, CT 06103

Los Angeles Kings
c/o Individual Player
P.O. Box 17013
Inglewood, CA 90308

Minnesota North Stars
Met Center
7901 Cedar Ave. South
Bloomington, MN 55425

Montreal Canadiens
Montreal, Quebec, Canada
2313 St. Katherine West.
413H IN2

New Jersey Devils
Fan Pack
P.O. Box 504
East Rutherford, NJ 07073

New York Islanders
Nassau Coliseum
Uniondale, NY 11553

New York Rangers
Public Relations
Madison Square Garden
Four Penn Plaza
New York, NY 10001

Philadelphia Flyers
The Spectrum-Pattison Pl.
Philadelphia, PA 15219

Pittsburgh Penguins
Civic Arena Gate #7
Pittsburgh, PA 15219

Quebec Nordiques
Colisee de Quebec
2205 Avenue de Colisee
Quebec, Quebec, Canada
GIL 4W7

San Jose Sharks
10 Almeden Blvd.
San Jose, CA 95113

St. Louis Blues
The Arena
5700 Oakland Ave.
St. Louis, MO 63110

Toronto Maple Leafs
Maple Leaf Gardens
60 Carlton St.
Toronto, Ontario, Canada
M5B ILI

Vancouver Canucks
Pacific Coliseum
100 North Renfrew St.
Vancouver, B.C., Canada
V5K 3N7

Washington Capitals
Capital Centre
Landover, MD 20786

Winnipeg Jets
Winnipeg Arena
15-1430 Maroons Rd.
Winnipeg, Manitoba,
Canada, R3G OL5

FREE   FREE   FREE

Something for nothing!! Hundreds of dollars' worth of items in each issue of **FREEBIES MAGAZINE.** 5 times a year, for more than 14 years, each issue has featured at least 100 FREE and low-postage-&-handling-only offers. Useful, informative, and fun items. Household information, catalogs, recipes, health and medical information, toys for the children, samples of everything from tea bags to jewelry—every offer of every issue is yours for FREE, or for a small postage and handling charge (never more than $2.00)!

Have you purchased a "Free Things" book before — only to find that the items were unavailable? That won't happen with FREEBIES — all of our offers are authenticated (and verified for accuracy) with the suppliers!

- -

☑ YES - Send me 5 issues for only $8.95 (save 30% off the cover price)

☐ Payment enclosed, or charge my   ☐ VISA   ☐ MasterCard

Card Number _ _ _ _ _ _ _ _ _ _ _ _ _ _ _ _   Exp. Date _ _ _ _

Name_____

Address_____

City_____ State _____ Zip_____

Daytime Phone

( )_____

(in case we have a question about your subscription)

Send to: FREEBIES MAGAZINE
1135 Eugenia Place, Carpinteria, CA 93013